C000005408

IMAGES OF ENGLAND

Sherborne &
Milborne Port

AERIAL PHOTOGRAPH OF MILBORNE PORT c. 1953. The many open spaces in this view of the southern half of the village have since been replaced with houses. Three Milborne Port churches can be seen; to the left is the parish church of St John the Evangelist, at the top is the Methodist church and, near the bottom in the middle, the Congregational church with schoolrooms which, until 1912, housed the old British School.

IMAGES OF ENGLAND

Sherborne & Milborne Port

Richard Brewer &
Richard Duckworth

NONSUCH

Detail from the photograph of Robert Adam's shop seen on page 10.

First published 1996
This new pocket edition 2006
Images unchanged from first edition

Nonsuch Publishing Limited
The Mill, Brimscombe Port,
Stroud, Gloucestershire, GL5 2QG
www.nonsuch-publishing.com

Nonsuch Publishing is an imprint of Tempus Publishing Group

British Library Cataloguing in Publication Data.
A catalogue record for this book is available from the British Library.

ISBN 1-84588-317-9

Typesetting and origination by Nonsuch Publishing Limited
Printed in Great Britain by Oaklands Book Services Limited

Contents

PEACE FETE IN MILBORNE PORT 9 AUGUST 1919. Happier days had arrived in Milborne Port at last. A fancy dress procession led by the Sherborne Military Band (bandmaster Mr W.J. Russell) wended its way down the High Street and into South Street. It is seen here passing the village cross adorned with flowers and the Union Jack in remembrance of those who fell in the Great War. The procession formed in Mr Richards' field opposite the National School and went to Ven Gardens for the Peace Celebration Fete and Sports Day. According to the official programme, the day started at 6.00 am with 'merry peals rung on the church bells', and in the afternoon there were sports for young and old with dancing on the croquet lawn. The day ended at 9.00pm with a fireworks display under the supervision of Mr E. Hann.

Opposite: CHEAP STREET, SHERBORNE, AT THE END OF THE NINETEENTH CENTURY. Although some of the shops have changed owners, e.g. on the corner of Long Street the 'Furnishing Ironmonger' is now a shoe shop and the chemist has changed from Dalwoods to the Abbey Pharmacy, from its general appearance the street is instantly recognizable.

Introduction

Old photographs are a silent record of the past, but in the hands of the skilled and knowledgeable they can be made to speak to us.

The authors of this book are both well-qualified to bring to life this new collection of historic images. Richard Brewer looks after the extensive photographic collection at Sherborne Museum and is himself a keen photographer. He went to school in Sherborne and has lived locally since retirement. He has used his darkroom skills to copy and enlarge some of the original negatives in the museum's collection to reveal details in them not previously visible. Richard Duckworth was born in Milborne Port and is the grandson of the local baker, Tom Coombs. He began collecting old photographs of his native village some fifteen years ago and now has a collection of about 5,000 photographs on which he has drawn for this book. He is well-known for his lectures and slide shows on old Milborne Port. Most of the photographs used here are published for the first time.

Milborne Port was a parliamentary borough until the Reform Act of 1832, returning two members. Its former prosperity is reflected in its fine buildings which are depicted in the photographs of this book. Woollen and flax mills contributed some of the wealth until the nineteenth century, when gloving (including tanning and dyeing) provided employment for many of the villagers. Sherborne has a long history as an ecclesiastical centre and a focus of commerce, industry and education. Gloving was also carried on here, along with silk-weaving, button and lace-making and brewing. It has managed to retain its prosperity without sacrificing too many of its lovely old buildings. Sherborne is one of the larger towns in Dorset and although Milborne Port is in Somerset, parts of the ancient parish extended into Dorset. The close proximity of the two communities ensured that they both shared similar economic influences and, being in a rural area, both have also relied heavily on agriculture.

The photographs in this book illustrate people at work, both in agriculture and industry, and at play, enjoying a variety of entertainments in their free time. Schools are depicted along with the different forms of transport available at the time.

It is reassuring to know that the old photographs in this book are well cared for and will be preserved for future generations to enjoy. Publications such as this make them readily accessible to everyone, to bring back memories to older inhabitants or to explore a lost world we never knew.

Ann Smith
Archivist
Sherborne Castle Estates
Spring 1996

One

Around Sherborne

SHERBORNE FROM THE SLOPES. A nineteenth-century print from a period just before the railway came to town.

ROBERT ADAMS' SHOP. The corner of Cheap Street and Half Moon Street, photographed by Adam Gosney, before demolition in 1891 to make way for road widening at the bottom of Cheap Street. On the left of the picture can be seen Bow Passage which led through to the Parade.

ADAMS' SHOP BEING DEMOLISHED IN 1891. By comparison it can be seen that the road here was widened by setting back the building line by some fifteen feet.

A DETAIL FROM ADAM GOSNEY'S GLASS PLATE NEGATIVE. This negative, now in the museum's collection, is of such high quality that it is possible to enlarge a portion of it to enable reading of the posters on the wall. It appears from this detail that the building was demolished in 1891, a date confirmed by Mr H.J. Seymour in his *Log Book of Sherborne from 634 to 1934*.

THE DEMOLITION GANG AND SOME INTERESTED SPECTATORS. This is another detail from the same negative once again showing its high quality. The feet in the top left-hand corner are those of Robert Adams himself who can be seen on the previous page at the top of the ladder. This has been confirmed by his great granddaughter who visited Sherborne in the Summer of 1995 and compared the picture with other photographs of Robert that she has in her possession.

A PICTURE FROM MATE'S 1903 'ILLUSTRATED SHERBORNE'. This shows the new building on the corner of Cheap Street and Half Moon Street that replaced Robert Adams' shop that was demolished in 1891. At this time it was occupied by the staff of the Urban District Council, owned by the Master and Brethren of the Almshouse and known as St Johns' House.

SHERBORNE URBAN DISTRICT COUNCIL 1953-54. Standing, left to right: S. Rose (Asst Clerk to the Council), W. Bown, R. Courage, C.E. Bean (Surveyor), E.J. Freeman (Clerk to the Council), C. Watt (Chairman), D. Stewart, Dr Pearson (Medical Officer of Health), ? Pinfield, E. Noake, A. Sweet. Front Row: A. Lugg, R. Gregory, Mrs R. McIntosh, Mrs W. Hewitt, P. Stretton.

BOW HOUSE, ORIGINALLY THE SUN INN. This was built in the sixteenth or seventeenth century and altered in the nineteenth and early twentieth centuries. It was acquired by Mr W.A. Dewey before the First World War and subsequently became the Central Temperance Hotel. At one time there was a shop at the right-hand side next to the Cross Keys, but this has been absorbed into the whole building. Once again known as Bow House, it is owned by Sherborne School and is the staff common room.

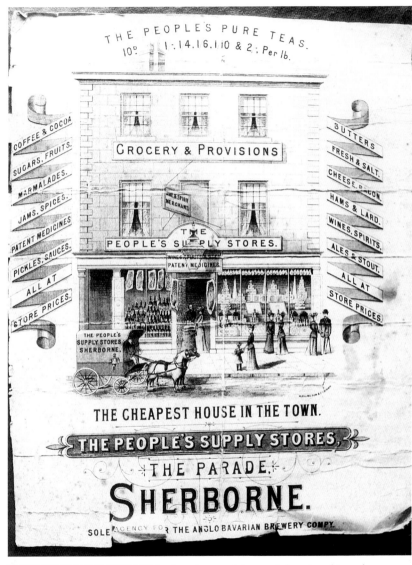

THE PEOPLE'S SUPPLY STORES. In the early years of the twentieth century this was known as Rodman's Stores but since the 1930s it has been the Three Wishes Restaurant. Parts of the building date from the seventeenth century although the front is from the nineteenth century.

Right: THE ABBEY CHURCH, THE
CONDUIT AND BOW HOUSE.
Viewed from Long Street in about
1874, the Sun Inn still has its plaster
rendering and the shop has a bow
front. Cheap Street has not yet been
widened at this point nor has the
Conduit been set back to its present
position. The Abbey clock is new,
having been presented by Mr George
Wingfield Digby and there are no
pinnacles on the Abbey tower; these
were erected in the 1880s.

Below: LONG STREET c. 1900.
Short's grocery is now occupied by a
ladies' and gentlemen's hairdresser.
On the left can be seen the Castle
Hotel and the Rose & Crown Inn,
now Rose Cottage.

CHILDS' CYCLE WORKS AND SHOP c. 1900. Originally the Sherborne Coffee Tavern, it was acquired by Edwin Childs towards the end of the nineteenth century. Later, it expanded to become Sherborne's first dealer in motor cars and the right hand window of the shop was hinged in order that a car could be taken into the shop and displayed. Eventually, Childs moved farther along the street and built showrooms and a garage which are still there, although the business has recently closed down and the site is due for development. The cycle business was taken over by the Hunt family and two brothers, Harry and David, continued to run it until well into the 1980s. The building is now occupied by estate agents, Gilyard Scarth, but the original Childs and Hunt frontage has been preserved.

THE UNION CONGREGATIONAL CHAPEL IN LONG STREET. This is so-called because when it was built in 1802 it marked the union of two smaller chapels from elsewhere in the town. In 1852 a schoolroom was built and both buildings survive, now acquired by Phillips, the Fine Arts Valuers and Auctioneers. Interiors have of course been much altered and all the headstones and memorials in the churchyard have been removed.

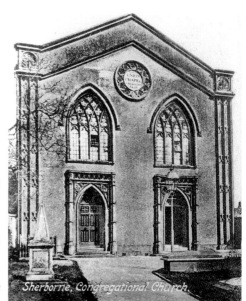

Sherborne, Congregational Church.

GIVE US THIS DAY OUR DAILY BREAD.

'ALL IS SAFELY GATHERED IN'. The interior of the Methodist Chapel in Cheap Street, decorated for Harvest Festival in the 1940s. It is now called the Cheap Street Church.

THE DORSETSHIRE BREWERY IN LONG STREET. This is a print of c. 1850. The brewery was established in 1796 and was originally owned by John Mills Thorne and later by the Baxter family. Brewing ceased in 1951 although malting continued until the 1970s. The building then remained empty, largely unused (although it was for a time a cheese store) and partially derelict until the 1980s when it was sympathetically redeveloped as high quality apartments and called The Maltings.

THE BREWERY YARD. Here are the coopers. Doubtless, the two gentlemen in bowler hats are their supervisors.

THE REAR OF THE DERELICT BREWERY BUILDING 1976. The brewery is seen here from Culverhayes car park, originally known as the Brewery Field. Although a large part of the brewery building remains as The Maltings, all the buildings in the foreground have gone and been replaced by Raleigh Court, a complex of apartments.

REMAINS OF A STONE-BUILT SHEEP DIP. Photographed by Gerald Pitman in what is now the Culverhayes car park in the late 1950s. The ends of the walls were decorated with carved stone angels, seen here badly eroded. Although not readily apparent from the photograph, each angel held a shield believed to be of similar design to those in the Abbey Church. A. B. Gourlay in his History of Sherborne School, says that before The Bath was built in 1873, the boys of the school bathed here!

T. E. VINCENT,

The Supply Stores

HALF MOON STREET and The DIGBY ROAD,

SHERBORNE.

Groceries,
Provisions,
Patent
Medicines,
Brushes,
Mats, &c.

Wines and
Spirits,
Ale and Stout
in Bottle or Cask,
Tobacco,
Cigars, &c.

Finest Indian, Ceylon and China Teas.

Coffee Fresh Roasted and Ground Daily

Detailed CASH PRICE LISTS on Application.

Above: HALF MOON STREET IN THE LATE NINETEENTH CENTURY. The Half Moon Commercial Hotel still has its archway inscribed, 'Posting and ...' indicating that at one time it had post horses for hire. From the right of the picture are: Cross the ironmongers, the Half Moon Hotel, Dingley's the drapers and Phillips & Handover's department store. The Half Moon was rebuilt in 1935 with the result that Cross's and Dingley's stores were demolished.

Left: AN EARLY ADVERTISEMENT FOR VINCENT'S STORES. This shop was on the corner of Half Moon Street and Digby Road and was later owned by Carter's but was still 'the' grocery store of Sherborne. It became Sherborne's first food supermarket owned by Mr R. Hamblin and was eventually taken over by Gateway. It closed when Somerfield's much larger supermarket was built and has now been converted into smaller units containing the Tourist Information Centre and shops, while upstairs is the Abbey Business Centre. The whole building is now known as Tilton Court.

THE CHURCH HOUSE IN HALF MOON STREET IN THE 1930s. This shop was occupied by John Isaacs with a tobacconists on the right, and the area on the left, which is discreetly curtained off, was the hairdressers. The whole of this area is now the Church House Gallery restaurant and tea rooms. The iron bracket supporting the Ladies' and Gentlemen's hairdressing sign is still there, although the sign itself has long since gone. This is a rare surviving example of a building built by the church in which secular entertainments such as theatre performances could be held. It certainly dates from the sixteenth century and may be older.

JOHN ISAACS,

Half Moon St., Sherborne

HAIRDRESSER AND PERFUMER.

—

Ladies' Hairdressing and Manicure Saloons.

Chiropody.

Hairwork of every description made on the premises.

Toilet requisites from best English and Foreign houses.

Competent male and female assistants in attendance.

CIGAR MERCHANT AND IMPORTER.

—

Large selection of high-class Cigars and Cigarettes always in stock.

Agent for all best Briar Pipe Manufacturers.

Special quotations given for Cigarettes in quantities of 500 and upwards.

We always guarantee our goods to be perfectly fresh.

JOHN ISAACS' ADVERTISEMENT IN A DIRECTORY OF 1903.

Sherborne, Cheap Street.

COOMBS'
RESTAURANT
20th Century Establishment
BUILT IN DELIGHTFUL OLD WORLD STYLE
CHEAP ST., SHERBORNE

CHEAP STREET IN THE LATE 1920s. Coombs' bakery on the left also contained a florist and a restaurant, but in 1935 it was completely rebuilt by Mr William Coombs, the owner. The picture below is copied from a publicity brochure that he produced at the time. His sons, George and Arthur, ran the business between them but after Arthur's death in 1958 and George's retirement in 1962, it closed and the building sold firstly to World Stores (who never developed it) and then to Woolworths who are still there today.

FREEMAN'S 'THE SPORTS HOUSE' IN CHEAP STREET, MID-1960s. This shop was opened in the early 1950s by E.J. Freeman, a retired county cricketer, who was also cricket coach to the boys of Sherborne School. The building dates from either the end of the eighteenth or beginning of the nineteenth century. No longer a sports shop, it is now the Dorset Music House.

LOWMAN & SONS,

The noted Sherborne Tailors and Outfitters.

Hunting, Shooting, Cycling, Golfing, Clericals & Liveries.
Also Ladies' Costumiers.

A TRIAL ORDER SOLICITED.

Cheap Street, SHERBORNE.

AN OLD BUILDING WITH A MODERN FRONT. Behind the shop front remains a seventeenth-century building. Mr Charles Lowman established this business in 1876, although the 1834 map in Sherborne Museum shows evidence of a shop here long before this. It is now the men's outfitters run by Dunn & Co.

HALF MOON FIELD. This was given to the town by Mr F.J.B. Wingfield Digby in memory of his father and in 1906 the surplus of the money raised by the 1905 Pageant was used to lay out the public gardens known ever since as the Pageant Gardens. The railway station can be seen in the background.

HALF MOON FIELD. The field was also used as the Pack Monday Fairground from about 1820 to 1905. This picture, from about 1900, shows the Sherborne Military Band standing in front of a steel open-topped bandstand with the Digby Hotel in the background.

THE EARLY STAGES OF LAYING OUT THE GARDENS. The field was known to be very marshy and reports exist of planks having to be laid to enable the bandsmen to walk to the bandstand. It is known that clinker from the nearby gasworks was used to make the ground more firm and from this picture it would seem that drains were laid and stone spread.

THE PAGEANT GARDENS AFTER COMPLETION. The Digby Hotel stands proudly in the background. On the far right of the picture may just be seen the Turkish field gun which had been captured by 'B' Squadron of the Dorset Yeomanry in Palestine on 15 November 1917 under the command of Major F.J.B. Wingfield Digby. The gun was presented to the town and placed in the gardens where it stayed for some years before being moved to its present site in the grounds of Sherborne Castle.

THIS GARDEN COMMEMORATES
THE SHERBORNE PAGEANT OF 1905
MOTHER OF ALL PAGEANTS
INVENTED AND DIRECTED BY
LOUIS NAPOLEON PARKER
AND JOYOUSLY PERFORMED
BY MEN AND WOMEN AND CHILDREN
OF SHERBORNE AND THE NEIGHBOURHOOD
AND BY THE MASTERS AND BOYS
OF SHERBORNE SCHOOL
TO THE GLORY OF GOD
AND IN CELEBRATION OF THE
TWELVE HUNDREDTH ANNIVERSARY
OF THE FOUNDING OF THE
BISHOPRIC TOWN AND SCHOOL
BY SAINT EALDHELM
A.D. 705

THE PLAQUE WHICH COMMEMORATES THE SHERBORNE PAGEANT. In July 1925, Mr Louis N. Parker, the Pageant Master who wrote and produced it, returned to Sherborne to unveil a block of stone placed in the gardens inscribed with the same wording as seen in this picture. However, over the years its condition deteriorated so much that it was removed and replaced by this plaque.

CASTLETON IN THE EARLY TWENTIETH CENTURY. The Old Castle is in the background. Very little has changed since, although the fence on the left has gone and from this viewpoint it is no longer possible to see the church because of the height of the surrounding trees.

CASTLETON FROM THE OBORNE ROAD 1900. This shows Raleigh Lodge and the railway bridge which dates from 1859. The field in the foreground is Miller's Mead. Castleton is an especially interesting part of Sherborne, not just because of its church and proximity to the Old Castle, but because it was one of the two old boroughs, the other being Newland. At one time this was part of the original Salisbury to Exeter road.

NOTICE IS HEREBY GIVEN,

THAT THE INSPECTORS APPOINTED

For Lighting the Town of
SHERBORNE.

Under the provisions of an Act passed in the 3d and 4th Years of the Reign of his present Majesty King William the Fourth intituled " An Act to repeal an Act of the Eleventh Year of his late Majesty King George the Fourth, for the Lighting and Watching of Parishes in England and Wales, and to make other provisions in lieu thereof," will hold their respective **MEETINGS** at the *Grand Jury Rooms* —

in Sherborne — — — — — — — —

on the **FIRST MONDAY** in every **MONTH**, at Noon, when and where any Inhabitant, rated to the Relief of the Poor of the said Town, may appear and prefer any matter of complaint he may think proper to make, concerning any thing done by force, or in pursuance, or under pretence of, the provisions of the said Act.

Signed, by Order of the Inspectors,

Malter H. Sher

Sherborne, *November 7th 1836.*

J. PENNY, JOURNAL OFFICE, SHERBORNE.

Left: ANNOUNCING THE INTENTION TO LIGHT THE STREETS 1836. Although it does not say so, this refers to street lighting by gas.

Below: THE GASWORKS IN THEIR HEYDAY. Seen here are the condensers and the retort house. Note the date 1864.

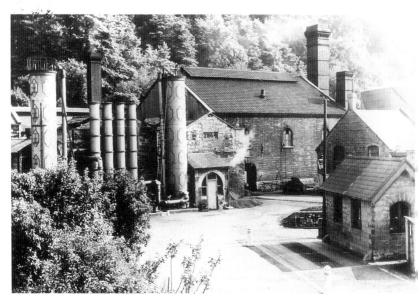

SOME OF THE GASWORKS' STAFF c. 1900. Centre front is Mr Cowling, the manager, flanked by Messrs Newman and Sansom. The man wearing the beard behind is Mr Burgess, whose son had a hairdressing business in Milborne Port.

A CEREMONY TO MARK NATIONALISATION OF GAS IN 1949. The stoker in conversation with the British Gas Board official is 'Taffy' Thomas who rose to the position of foreman before he retired.

SOUTH STREET 1937. This was the year of the Coronation of King George VI and Queen Elizabeth and, in common with the rest of the country, Sherborne streets and buildings were decorated with red, white and blue bunting, Union flags, crowns etc. Chaffin's, seen here, was an old-established photographer's family business which had been in Sherborne since the middle 1800s and he no doubt felt that his premises should be second to none in display. The lettering under the crown reads 'Long Live Their Majesties'.

SOUTH STREET NEAR THE RAILWAY CROSSING IN THE EARLY 1900s. The photograph is captioned 'The Milk Factory'. Originally a silk mill stood near this site, called Melmoth's although the 1834 map and terrier of Sherborne describe it as the Middle Silk Mill. The milk factory was originally owned by Surrey Dairies who manufactured Cow & Gate dried milk products there. Eventually this became part of United Dairies of London, the forerunners of Unigate (see p. 79).

A NINETEENTH-CENTURY PRINT OF THE YEATMAN HOSPITAL. Built in 1864 as a memorial to the late Revd H.F. Yeatman of Stock House, Stock Gaylard, near Lydlinch, it opened to patients in 1866. It has been extended several times since then, most recently in 1994, and although most of the original building is embedded somewhere in the present structure, it is in no way recognizable from this picture.

THE MEDICAL AND NURSING STAFF IN 1933. Back row, includes: Nurses Bowden, Tucker, Pocock, Lemon, Miss Warleigh (physiotherapist), Nurses Dawson and Jeans, Mr J. Dingley (secretary). Centre row: Dr G.R. Rickett, Sister Schilbach, Dr Whittingdale Snr, Miss Kearvell (matron), Dr T. McCarthy, Sister Taylor, Dr Whittingdale Jnr. Front row: Probationer Nurses Watley, -?-, Dufosée, Fothergill, Fletcher.

THE ALMSHOUSE. More correctly called the Hospital of St John the Baptist and St John the Evangelist, this building dates back to the fifteenth century, although it was altered and enlarged in the nineteenth. This is the earlier part, originally the main entrance, fronting Trendle Street. Of special interest in this 1939 picture are the Victorian iron posts and rails lining the kerb, whose finials are a bishop's mitre, the badge of the Almshouse. Due to the ravages of time and traffic they had to be replaced in 1995 and by the generosity of the Master and Brethren, Sherborne Museum now has one of the original posts in its collection. The inmate leaning on the rail is dressed in the uniform which it was obligatory to wear until after the Second World War. The lower picture shows sixteen 'poor men' and six 'poor women' in 1893 with the matron. Up to eight women could be admitted so perhaps there were two vacancies, although the men's quarters are shown to be fully occupied.

SHERBORNE CASTLE,
SEP. 5TH 1906.

THE FRONT OF SHERBORNE 'NEW' CASTLE IN SEPTEMBER 1906. These decorations had been erected to celebrate the coming-of-age of Mr F.J.B. Wingfield Digby. The lettering over the arch reads 'Long Live Our Squire'. There are a number of other photographs taken at the time which show that the main entrance from the New Road was also decorated to mark the occasion.

THE BLACKMORE VALE HUNT. Naturally, hunting was very popular and the Hunt frequently met at the castle. It was quite usual for local people to attend as it must have been a very colourful occasion. This picture, 3 November 1913, gives a very clear idea of the large number of onlookers. At this time Col. F.J.B. Wingfield Digby was the Master.

'UP TO LODGE' 1907. Although no records appear to exist as to when this custom commenced, it was, and still is, a tradition that the people of Sherborne go to the Estate yard at 9.00 am on Christmas morning to receive money, the personal gift of the Squire. A hundred years ago it was 'two bright pennies', in the 1930s it was four old pence and at present it is a 20p coin, still given at the same place.

A WINGFIELD DIGBY FAMILY GARDEN PARTY IN THE 1890s. In the centre, wearing a light coloured bowler hat, is Mr J.K.D. Wingfield Digby. On his right is Charlotte, his second wife, and in front of them is Freddie, his son by his first marriage, whose coming-of-age celebrations were seen in an earlier picture.

SHERBORNE PARK 6 JULY 1893. The Duke of York (subsequently King George V) married Princess May of Teck and to celebrate the occasion, Mr J.K.D. Wingfield Digby MP provided a treat in the castle grounds for the Amalgamated Sunday Schools of Sherborne. The very large numbers pictured here give some idea of the strength of the Sunday School and Bible Class movements at this time.

SKATING ON SHERBORNE LAKE IN THE 1890s. The Squire shared the castle grounds with the people of the town. Whenever there was a hard winter and the lake froze, the townspeople were allowed to skate on it. A notice was placed at the lodge gates and at the Digby estate office in Cheap Street to inform everybody that 'the ice is bearing'.

THE DORSET YEOMANRY (VOLUNTEER) REGIMENT ANNUAL CAMP. The Regiment
often held its summer training camp in Sherborne Park and these pictures of about 1900 show
the bridge-building platoon and their pontoon bridge at the eastern end of the lake. Here
are Lieutenant W.H. Baxter and his men of whom the following have been identified: Sgt J.J.
Dalwood and Privates A.L. and W. Clarke, G. Hann, G. Jacobs, C. Lane, W. Maber,
S. Penny, J. Read, H. Russell, ? Plympton and ? Simmonds.

WARSHIP WEEK NOVEMBER 1941. During the Second World War it became the practice for districts throughout the country to hold fund-raising weeks to help finance the war effort. These weeks were themed, such as Spitfire Week to raise money to buy fighter aircraft, and Warship Week pictured here which took place from 1st to 8th November 1941. The final amount raised was £179,556. This is the lower end of Cheap Street. The outfitter's shop on the right was N.E. Stickland, the building now occupied by the Bristol & West Building Society. In 1962, following the closure of Coombs' Restaurant, Woolworths took over the site. The shop they vacated became a supermarket, latterly Lo-Cost, now closed.

THE CORONATION OF QUEEN ELIZABETH II 1953. The same part of Cheap Street twelve years later on the occasion of the Queen's Coronation. At this date, there seems to have been very few, if any, changes in ownership of the shops.

UNVEILING OF THE WAR MEMORIAL 11 NOVEMBER 1921. The Earl of Shaftesbury performed the ceremony. The cost was raised by public subscription, although at the time of the dedication the whole sum was still to be raised. The *Western Gazette* of 18 November 1921 reported that four nurses were in attendance to take a collection from the many hundreds who attended the ceremony. Four troopers of the Dorset Regiment, P.H. Bown, F. Johnson, A.H. Lugg and D. Welham, stood with bowed heads around the memorial during the dedication service carried out by many local clergy and led by Bishop Joscelyne, Archdeacon of Sherborne. The dedication was attended by relatives of the fallen and was followed by a parade of 400 ex-servicemen and local organisations.

THE HOME GUARD DRUM AND FIFE BAND 1939-45. Back row, left to right: Ron Dyke, L. Crane, ? Schumacher. Second row: Gerald Smith, ? White, Eric Noake, Jack Foot, Jack Lugg. Third row: ? Amens, Irwin Crocker, George Alford, ? Chant, Doug Harris. Front row, with drums: Ray Davis, -?-.

Two

Around Milborne Port

TOWN HALL. MILBORNE PORT.

THE TOWN HALL c. 1906 Also known as the Market House, it has had a variety of uses over the years, from market house to school (from 1836 to 1854).

THE OLD VICARAGE c. 1910. This was the second one to be built in Milborne Port and was situated on the south side of Sherborne Road. Built in 1870 by Sir William Medlycott, it replaced the former vicarage that stood in the churchyard near the spot where the war memorial now stands. In 1937 it was replaced by the present vicarage and is now a hotel and restaurant.

CRACKMORE AVENUE c. 1929. The A30 looking west towards Sherborne and showing the Traveller's Rest. The Renault car on the left is emerging from Goathill Road. At this time Mr Harold Clark's garage had not been built. There is an almost exactly similar example of the Traveller's Rest lamp standard still in front of the parish church.

GAINSBOROUGH c. 1920. Looking northwards up Gainsborough, we see a block of houses which were rebuilt after the 1905 fire that left many homeless, including Mr Jackson the butcher (see page 52). These houses remained until about 1937 when they were demolished.

GAINSBOROUGH c. 1905. Moving further up the road, and past the corner seen in the photograph above, is a group of three shops. Nothing is recalled about the top two, although in this picture they look as if they were no longer in use then, but Mr H.E. Luffman's shop was a general store and many local people will remember a shop here until well into the 1970s. Note the children, possibly in their Sunday best, posing for the photographer.

NEWTOWN, ALSO KNOWN AS BLUETOWN c. 1910. These houses were built by Lord Darlington between 1818 and 1822 to gain votes for the Liberal, or 'Blue' party, hence the name. The houses were built so badly that for many years after, much money was spent on repairing them. During the 1920s and 30s a number of small shops and businesses were run in Newtown from just one room in the house. This photograph shows the old Pump House, long since demolished. Next to it, just out of view, was a small Mission Room used by all denominations, last used for services in 1943. Its small altar is now in the south transept of the parish church.

NEWTOWN c. 1905. The result of one of many fires that occurred in the village in the early years of the twentieth century. No doubt the Milborne Port fire brigade needed assistance from Sherborne as they only had a hand pump at the time. The people posing for the camera certainly had a sense of humour; behind the man on the right someone has written 'Cheap, To Let'!

BAUNTON'S ORCHARD. A 1970s view of the road looking down towards South View. Before this time, these houses commanded a wonderful outlook from their high position, to the southern part of the village, but in the present day grazing cows have been replaced by new housing estates.

SOUTH VIEW. When the council houses here were built in about 1927, it made a quick through route for the many people who lived in the top part of the village and worked in the glove factory. Before this road was opened, they would have had to wheel their bicycles or walk across a field into Wick Road on their way to work.

KINGSBURY BRIDGE c. 1920. On the left is Manor Farm and this road went on to Kingsbury Mill and another small farm owned by the Southcombe family. The bridge was built in 1856, replacing a ford, and cost £30. The stone came from Toomer Quarry. In the foreground is the footbridge leading to the Dairy House and the cowstalls owned by Mr David Shingleton of Manor Farm.

KINGSBURY MILL c. 1910. This was one of the many mills that lay on the course of the River Gascoigne that flowed through the village. Many years ago it was diverted to run behind the mill in order to operate its corn mill, but in the early 1930s, when the water wheel was no longer in use, a swimming pool was constructed in the mill pool and it was cemented round. In the summer changing tents were also erected. The river has now reverted to its original course in front of the mill. The mill was also a bakehouse for many years and during the Second World War, dances were held on the upper floor.

KINGSBURY c. 1931. Milborne Port fire brigade in action on a wash-day Monday morning. Mrs Brixey had stoked the copper to heat the water when sparks from the fire set the thatched roof alight. The fire spread to the thatched roofs of Manor Farm Cottages, leaving the Brixeys and Mr and Mrs Hinks temporarily homeless. The captain of the fire brigade at this time was Mr George Gosney.

MILBORNE PORT FIRE BRIGADE. Standing outside the fire station in Higher Gunville in July 1940 with a trailer pump used during the 1939-45 war are; back row, left to right: R. Hansford, V. Gosney, A. Hallett, W. Ham, V. Starling. Front row: G. Gosney (captain), F. Abbott (vice-captain), L. Foyle, H. Hinks, G. Jeans, B. Abbott, W. Hyde, L. Cory, R. Raymond. Later, the fire station was moved to the back of Cross House in North Street and the brigade was finally disbanded in 1961.

RUSSELL PLACE c. 1920. Maude Chant is in her father's donkey cart pulled by 'Joey'. Russell Place is a row of five pairs of houses, built in 1867 and named after the former owner of the land. Little has changed over the years except that the gardens in front of the houses are much smaller. There were once gates at the entrance to Russell Place and the last person through them at night had to shut them.

KINGSBURY FROM THE AIR c. 1952. An interesting aerial view of the industrial part of Milborne Port. It shows Ensor's glove factory and tannery as well as Silas Dyke's tannery. Next to the factory is the Methodist church, now converted into flats. In the centre of the picture is the old gasworks and on the right, Kingsbury Regis and Manor Farm, home of the Shingleton family for many years.

THE CHURCH SCHOOL c. 1920. One of the first buildings to be seen when entering the village along the A30 from Sherborne is the old church (or National) school. It was built at a cost of more than £2,000 by Sir William Medlycott of Ven House and opened to pupils in July 1864, replacing the school held in the old market house. The tower and spire were a later addition in 1878 and the clock was given by the people of Milborne Port.

SHERBORNE ROAD c. 1920. Standing in the middle of the road with a group of children is the village policeman, PC Gibbs. The thatched cottage on the right caught fire in the 1950s and was later converted into a bungalow. The road to the left is Rosemary Lane (now Rosemary Street).

Left: PARROTT & TADGELL. An advertisement taken from the parish magazine of May 1948 which makes interesting reading because nearly all the businesses from Milborne and Sherborne which advertised there have long since closed. In fact, the only advertisers still in existence are from Sherborne, Messrs C.B. Brett and the Abbey Bookshop.

Below: SANSOMES HILL c. 1904. A quite different scene from today's busy roads. A horse and cart proceed along what is now the A30 past a turning to the left which leads to St John's church. On the left of the picture can just be seen the top of the blacksmith's shop which was for many years run by Mr Jimmy Merrett.

Right: THE CHURCH OF ST JOHN THE EVANGELIST. This parish church is thought to have been built around 1066 and during the next few hundred years additions, alterations and strengthening work have followed. A major restoration was undertaken between 1867 and 1869 by Mr A. Reynolds who also built the church school. This photograph shows the church floodlit on the occasion of the 1957 Parish Mission.

Below: THE INTERIOR OF ST JOHN'S CHURCH. The inside of this beautiful Church can be seen to full effect in this view looking east towards the chancel which is the oldest part of the church. The fine Harrison organ is seen here on the left of the picture before it was moved to the south transept in the 1930s. It was dedicated in 1912 to the memory of the Revd C.H.P. Crawfurd, a former vicar, and cost about £800. It was moved again in the late 1960s to its present position at the west end of the church.

Above: THE TOWN STEPS, HIGH STREET c. 1908. At one time, this end of the High Street was a very busy part of the village. The first house on the left was Miss Stone's private school, next was T. Thring the draper, then Mr J. Hearne the ironmonger and Calder's butchers shop. Behind the butchers was the slaughterhouse, the animals being driven up through Higher Gunville from a field near the glove factory known as 'the killing field'. Near the draper's shop was the first village post office, burnt down in the late 1800s.

Left: THE OLD MARKET CROSS. For hundreds of years the old Cross was the centre of village life. From here, proclamations were read and market tolls collected. It was originally situated in the centre of the village on the crossroads by the Town Hall, but in 1959 it was moved to its present position seen here, near the site of the old bandstand, close to the parish church.

HIGH STREET 1905. An old postcard which provides a view of the many changes seen in the High Street over the last 91 years. On the right is Tom Coombs' bakery and shop. The next shop was also owned by the Coombs family but was later sold for £50 and became the general provision store owned by Mr George Stagg. On the left the creeper-clad building was opened in 1875 as a branch of Stuckey's Bank of Langport. Next to it, the building now the post office, was Dr Empson's surgery. This picture also gives a good display of Edwardian fashions.

THE GARDEN OF REMEMBRANCE c. 1960. Originally built in 1847 as a fives court or ball court by Sir W.C. Medlycott 'for the promotion of healthy recreation for the working classes', it later became a Garden of Remembrance to commemorate those inhabitants of the village who died in the two World Wars. Beyond can be seen the Westminster Bank House, formerly the site of Stuckey's Bank (see above).

HIGH STREET c. 1904. The second door on the left, site of the old police station, later became Jackson's new butcher's shop (see page 41). The large door next to it is the entrance to the ancient Guildhall, the ground floor of which was once used as a jail. Opposite is The King's Head Hotel, formerly known as either The Tippler or The Tippling Philosopher.

THE GUILDHALL, HIGH STREET. This has been the meeting place for many years of the Commonalty Charity Lands and also a reading room. The Liberal Party used it as their committee rooms in the early 1900s. In the picture is the fine high-backed Magisterial Chair used by Thomas Medlycott when he 'tried for unruly and violent conduct in Sherborne, Bampfylde-Moor Carew, known as the King of the Beggars'. Some fine oil paintings, the work of Miss E. Medlycott, can also be seen.

THE OLD FIRE ENGINE. This was given to the Borough of Milborne Port by T. Medlycott Esq. of Ven in 1733. For a time it was kept in the parish church and one amusing story tells of it being trundled up the aisle while a service was in progress, much to the agitation of the Revd West, particularly as most of the congregation left to see the fire! Posing in the 1930s beside it is a group of Milborne Port men in period costume, left to right: Joe Giles, G. Gosney, F. Abbott, B. Abbott, Jack Gosney, Frank Penny, Harry Hinks and Cecil Skyvington.

SOUTH STREET c. 1910. This view looks north through the top half of South Street towards the old market cross. On the left can be seen the barber's pole of Hedley Dyke. On the right is part of the Town Hall and houses belonging to the Commonalty Charity, one of which was a grocer's shop run for many years by Mr and Mrs A. Chant who would also deliver paraffin to your door.

SOUTH STREET c. 1910. The thatched cottage on the left was renovated and converted to a bungalow in 1935. Behind the man standing in the road, the end house in the terrace, was the police station, having moved from the High Street. At the bottom of the hill was the old museum, now a private dwelling. On the right, behind the person standing, there were some old stables. Horses used during the Great War were housed there.

BROOKSIDE c. 1972. This interesting picture shows the old museum from the area called 'Between the Waters'. The museum housed many of Ven House's relics from before the Second World War. The long low-roofed building to the right of centre is the old laundry and workhouse, the roof ventilators of which can clearly be seen. The pegged-out land is now Brookside and Cannon Court farmhouse can just be seen on the right.

CHURCH STREET c. 1960. Over the wall, along the front of this picture, were housed the headquarters of the Milborne Port tennis club. In the 1930s, the Club had two hard courts and a small pavilion on land behind the bakehouse owned by Mr Tom Coombs. At this time tennis was very popular and there were twelve more courts around the village.

THE CONGREGATIONAL CHAPEL c. 1910. An inside view, looking east and showing the organ that was replaced in the 1970s by one from Wincanton. The chapel was built in 1844, replacing a much smaller one on the same site. The present chapel closed in 1991 due to falling numbers and the high cost of much needed repairs. It has subsequently been renovated and now houses the English Organ School and Museum and holds a fine collection of organs and other musical instruments.

AROUND THE WEIGHBRIDGE c. 1936. The old post office is to the left of the car. The first one had been by the town steps (see p. 50). The weighbridge, situated near the house on the right, was operated from the Queen's Head (in front of the car) for many years by the Tizzard family at a charge of three old pence per waggon.

e oldest and best
Dyers.

Myra's Journal.

Milborne Port, *Sep 29* 190 0

(SOMERSET).

Mr Leger

Bought of N. E. STICKLAND,

General Draper, Outfitter, &c.

DRESSMAKING.   **MILLINERY.**

BOOTS AND SHOES.

Catalogues and Price
Lists Free.

SHIRT MAKING A SPECIALITY

Regular Despatches to
he works carriage free.

Bespoke and Mourning Orders at the Shortest Notice.

Branch Establishment :—Cheap Street, Sherborne.

Sep 29 Cash on A/ct — .7 0

N.E. STICKLAND, OUTFITTERS. A billhead of 1900 from this business which also had a larger shop in Sherborne. In Milborne Port their shop was by the weighbridge and was rented from the Commonalty Charity. It was L-shaped, on two floors, and the Stickland family lived next door. Two separate businesses occupy the building now.

EAST STREET c. 1920. A peaceful village scene as two ladies and young children with a bicycle pose for the camera. There has been little change otherwise in this view over the last seventy five years. This was once part of the main road to London, running across the fields by Gospel Ash Farm and joining the present day A30 at the top of Toomer Hill.

LONDON ROAD c. 1955. This postcard view of that year shows how little the road has changed. The Queen's Head was in the hands of the Tizzard family for about eighty seven years from 1868 to 1955. First of all, Mr George Tizzard was landlord, followed by his son Bert, whose wife Dorothy continued to run the pub after his death in 1946. Beyond the pub is the grocer's shop owned at the time by P.W. Agate and beyond that the cottages on London Road.

VEN HOUSE c. 1910. Ven House, one of the most outstanding buildings in the village, is believed to have been built between 1720 and 1725 by James Medlycott. The house probably incorporated a smaller one built earlier by his father, Thomas Medlycott, between 1698 and 1700. In 1836 extensive alterations were carried out to the interior. The house was the home of the Medlycott family, except for a short time during the Second World War, until 1957.

AN AERIAL VIEW OF VEN c. 1938. An early aerial view of Ven House. In the foreground can be seen the front of the house with its fine terrace and gardens. Under the terrace, the River Yeo (or Gascoigne, as it is known locally) runs on its way to Sherborne Lake. The kitchen gardens are on the right. An avenue of trees ran from East Hill to the house and on towards Goathill Road, but sadly they were felled in 1967. Although they were replaced, these too have perished, suffering from the hot dry summer of 1976 and Dutch Elm Disease.

NORTH STREET c. 1910. Here we see the ancient Market Cross which was moved in 1959. The building on the left with trees in front of it is Stagg & Trott's glove factory which later, after renovation, became used as the Conservative Club. Across the road is Cross House behind which at one time was a factory for weaving and later glove making.

E.J. HANN, NORTH STREET c. 1908. Ned Hann, in the centre, poses with his son Geoff on his left. On his right is Mr Abbott. Hann's was a carpenters and joiners as well as undertakers business. Many local folk took their last journey on his bier, which is still kept in the cemetery chapel. The old Stagg & Trott glove factory, which closed in 1911, is on the left.

Methodist Church, Milborne Port

Above: NORTH STREET c. 1910. The Victoria Hall, behind the man on the left, was erected in 1887 by Silas Dyke. It was equipped with a stage and was used for many parish functions and was said to seat 250 people. The large building on the right was Silas Dyke's glove factory, built in 1858, and reputed to have made the highest grade gloves in the country.

Left: THE METHODIST CHURCH c. 1935. Built in 1866, the first service was held in this church in April of that year. Originally built to accommodate 480 it was later altered and the numbers seated slightly reduced. To the north there was a large schoolroom together with a set of classrooms used by the Sunday schools. At one time there were in excess of 290 children on the Sunday school roll. Some old Milbornians said that in the early 1900s if you went to church in the morning you didn't go in the evening, to give other people a chance! The church closed in October 1988 and has now been converted into flats. The present congregation can now be accommodated in the nearby refurbished manse which has meeting rooms in it.

THE INTERIOR OF THE METHODIST CHURCH. A picture taken before the building was made into flats. Here we are looking north and towards the main schoolroom, where the Boys' Brigade met for many years. There was also a small chapel, a vestry, and a kitchen. Not seen in this picture is a balcony and just below the organ was another, smaller, balcony used by the choir.

MILBORNE WICK CHURCH c. 1930. This little church, about one and a quarter miles from Milborne Port but within its parish, stands in the middle of this pretty little hamlet, surrounded by farms and close to the old mill which still has a large overshot waterwheel. Built in 1891, its first service was held on 21 October that year. It can seat approximately 50 people.

THE DRESSING YARD OF SILAS DYKE'S FACTORY c. 1928. A photograph taken from the footpath leading to Bullen's Ground shows how much has changed in the last sixty years. Housing now fills the green fields, seen on the top left. From the top middle to the top right of the picture are Baunton's Orchard and South View.

WEST VIEW c. 1950. These council houses, built in the 1920s, command a fine view looking over Kingsbury to the western edge of the village. Behind these houses are the Memorial Playing Fields which were opened in May 1955 after members of local youth organisations had worked hard to clear the fields of tons of stones.

Three

At Work

THE SHERBORNE JOURNAL. This was the town's 'local' paper in the nineteenth century.

Left: THE SHERBORNE SILK MILLS IN 1912. In the eighteenth and nineteenth centuries there were a number of local factories producing thrown silk. However, by this time West Mill, seen here, was weaving fine quality silks. It was situated in Ottery Lane (once known as Factory Lane). This photograph records the installation of a new engine. From left to right are: W. Longbottom (in charge of installation), W. Clarke, W. Ogden, Mr Wright Snr (owner of the mills), Mrs Wright, Mr Foster (whose company supplied the engine), Mr Ogden Snr (weaving overlooker), Mr Warry (engine driver), Mr Howe (warehouse manager), Mr and Mrs Wright Jnr.

Below: THE EMPLOYEES OF THE SILK MILLS IN 1905. This is one of a pair of photographs from Sherborne Museum which give a good idea of the number of people employed at the mills.

THOMAS ENSOR'S FACTORY AND SILAS DYKE'S DRESSING YARD, MILBORNE PORT c. 1950. This aerial view clearly shows the industrial centre of the village. These two sites were separated by the River Gascoigne which runs left to right immediately below the two large white buildings seen centre and right of the picture. These buildings were rebuilt after a fire in 1947. Also seen in the photograph is the old Methodist church with its fine spire.
The Paddock Walk area, to the bottom of the picture, is now totally filled with new housing.

THOMAS ENSOR'S, WEST HILL, MILBORNE PORT c. 1930. In 1900 Messrs Southcombe and Sons of Tintinhull bought the business of Thomas Ensor, and continued to trade under that name. Until the 1930s Mr Bernard Southcombe travelled once a year to Port Elizabeth, South Africa in order to have first choice of the sheepskins from the huge warehouses there. This picture shows the main office and, left to right: Mr Stanley Southcombe, Mr John Clark, Mr Bernard Southcombe, Mr Hector Southcombe.

THOMAS ENSOR'S GLOVE FACTORY, THE FINISHING DEPARTMENT c. 1930. Many Milborne Port people will remember Charlie Luffman, who for years was a mainstay of the local Red Cross group, also Alec Davis who in later years had a fish and chip shop situated just below the church school. Here we see them with fellow workers in Thomas Ensor's finishing department, from left to right: Frank Woodley, Alfie Riggs, Charlie Luffman, Alec Davis, Sid Peters, Tom King, Tom Peters.

THOMAS ENSOR'S DYE HOUSE, MILBORNE PORT c. 1930. The dye house was part of the tannery yard operations. Conditions in this part of the process would not have been to the safety standards that apply today. At 8am, 1pm, 2pm and 6pm the old steam hooter could be heard around Milborne Port, announcing the start or finish of a shift. A mad rush of people then followed on bicycles, or on foot, either to or from work. This picture of the dye house shows, from left to right: Cliff Woodhouse, -?-, Stewart Woodhouse, Buffer Ham, -?-.

Right: CHIMNEY SWEEPS AT THOMAS ENSOR'S, MILBORNE PORT c. 1930. One job that had to be done on a regular basis was the sweeping of the factory chimneys and, by the look of this picture, it was a very dirty job indeed! Here we see the men who had just completed the task at Thomas Ensor's. Top row, left to right: Mr Jacobs, Mr King, Mr Spearing. Bottom row: Charlie Pullen, Mr A. Penny.

Below: THOMAS ENSOR'S MACHINE ROOM, MILBORNE PORT c. 1930. Standing at the back of this picture is Miss Newton the forewoman. Imagine the noise in this room as the twenty eight girls operated their treadle sewing machines, using different types of stitching known as 'prick seam', 'pique making' and 'brosser making'. All the hand sewing, and some machine work, was completed by outworkers. In 1914, Ensor's employed 201 factory workers and 370 outworkers. The output was between 800 and 1000 dozen gloves per week. The total wage bill for 1914 was £13,200.

THE SHERBORNE LAUNDRY. Built in 1901 by Canon F.B. Westcott, headmaster to serve the needs of Sherborne School, its full name was The Sherborne Steam Sanitary Laundry Co Ltd. It expanded to include the Preparatory School and then Sherborne School for Girls, and of course, the town. It remained the Sherborne Laundry until 1960 when it amalgamated with other West Country laundries to become the Guarantee Laundry, but since then other members of the group have closed, leaving Sherborne's laundry the only survivor. This picture of the staff was taken in 1915.

* Auntie Gertie (Tramp)

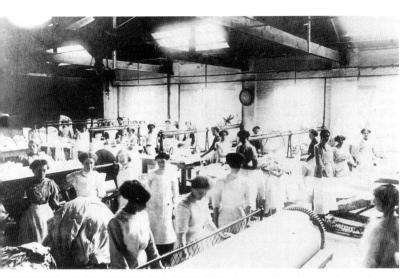

THE SHERBORNE LAUNDRY, IRONING ROOM. Taken at about the same time as the photograph on the previous page, this shows the 'calenders' as the giant ironing machines were called.

SHERBORNE LAUNDRY, BOILING ROOM 1932. From left to right are: A. Lambert, ? Batten, ? Smith, D. Redfern, T. Tothill (who eventually became engineer/manager), D. Watts, R. Lane, R. Hookings and H. Gosney.

JOINT MANAGING DIRECTOR AT SILAS DYKE'S c. 1930. An interesting picture from the 1930s, long before the introduction of computers and fax machines. Seen in his office is Mr T.E. Dyke, joint managing director of Silas Dyke's. On the wall is a photograph of Mr Silas Dyke who founded the firm in 1837. There is also a poster exhorting 'Buy British Gloves for Best Results'. Sadly, in later years, cheap foreign imports caused great problems for the local gloving industry.

SILAS DYKE'S NORTH STREET FACTORY, MILBORNE PORT c. 1935. Two girls entering Silas Dyke's creeper-clad factory in North Street. This factory building was built in 1858 and, sadly, closed down in 1984. The building remains largely intact today but is now converted into shops and flats. There has been glovemaking in the village since 1810 and in that time seventeen firms have started and folded. Silas Dyke's dressing yard was situated in Higher Kingsbury (see page 62).

SILAS DYKE'S MAIN CUTTING SHOP, MILBORNE PORT c. 1932. This 1930s photograph shows approximately half of Silas Dyke's North Street glove cutters. Silas Dyke's employed eighty to ninety people in its North Street factory, plus many outworkers. Another thiry five to forty were employed in their Kingsbury dressing yard. Left to right are: Frank Penny, Viv Gosney, Bill Hinks, Bill Gillard, Tom Burgess, Harry Hinks, Frank Fox, Jack Hann, John Trott, Stan Woodhouse.

SILAS DYKE'S GLOVE LINING AND FUR CUTTING DEPT., MILBORNE PORT c. 1932. In the 1930s fur-lined gloves were a luxury item and therefore expensive but they were but one of 480 different styles of glove on offer from Silas Dyke's North Street factory. Seen here is the glove lining and fur cutting department, one of many stages in glove making. Left to right are: Billy Pitman, Fritz (John) Cory, George Winter, Jim Bull, Charlie Davis.

PARSONS THE BUTCHERS IN CHEAP STREET, SHERBORNE 1928. This is believed to be the oldest family business in the street, if not in the town. The building dates back to 1840, although the shop front was altered after the 1939-45 war. The business was originally in the old shambles on the corner of South and Half Moon Streets, but moved to the present site in 1863. Members of staff are: George Willis, Jim Cheney, Mark Parsons (from whom the present owners are directly descended), Percy Bown, William Baker, ? Bishop, Joe Paul, Jack Parks. Between William Baker and the boy, Bishop, are notices regarding a bullock that Mr Parsons had purchased from the King at the Windsor Fatstock Show that year.

SOUTH STREET, SHERBORNE. Greenham's, another long established business, which is now no longer in existence. This picture is dated 1937 and among the staff here present are: G. Parkes, W. Durrant, H. Durrant and H. Pope, who was captain of the Abbey bellringers for many years.

STICKLAND & CO, GROCERS, MILBORNE PORT c. 1910. This is one of the oldest surviving shops in the village. It was situated in London Road and was mentioned in a directory published by the Somerset County Gazette in 1840. At that time, the shop was owned by Samuel Highmore who also ran a chemists and drugstore, possibly the shop to the right of the front door. This picture shows the shop in the ownership of Stickland & Co. who had it until the Second World War. Mr Stickland had a brother who was a draper and outfitter in the village and in Sherborne (see pp. 37 and 124).

GEORGE STAGG, GROCER, HIGH STREET, MILBORNE PORT c. 1935. Seen outside this shop is Mr Stagg's eldest daughter, Dorothy, who later became Mrs Spiller. Mr Stagg had a milk round as well as a grocery and general provisions shop. After the Second World War, the shop became a chemists, first run by Mr Tolman and then, for many years, by Mr and Mrs Tom Nussey.

DURRANT'S THE GROCERS, SHERBORNE. This is the site in Cheap Street now occupied by the Bristol & West Building Society (see page 37). Durrant's was a well-established family business which had, at one time, also been on the corner of Cheap and Long Streets.

DYER'S, CHEAP STREET, SHERBORNE. Dyer's took occupancy of the building in Cheap Street in about 1895 and this picture dates from that time. The business is still there although the front of the shop was rebuilt between the wars and bicycles are no longer sold. No member of the Dyer family has an interest in the business now, but it can surely claim to be another of the oldest in the town.

JAMES L. CANDY, CHEAP STREET, SHERBORNE. This old advertisement came from an early Directory of Sherborne, but apart from saying the shop was in Cheap Street, there is no clue in the book as to its exact location. However, it is possible to make an informed guess as to its whereabouts. The side of the street can be confirmed easily because the picture shows the street's slope and the general shape of the window and door, and the small ventilation grill at pavement level, all strongly suggest that it is the premises now occupied by Global Image.

James L. CANDY,

Monumental and General Mason,

Cheap Street, SHERBORNE

HEADSTONES, CROSSES, LEDGERS TABLETS, CURBING LETTER CUTTING Marble Shop Fittings Sanitary Appliances &c. in MARBLE, STONE or GRANITE.

MR RICKARD'S SHOP IN CHEAP STREET, SHERBORNE. This could be the same shop that is occupied by James Candy, above, but if it is it appears to have been extended to take in next door and here, in 1920, it is owned by Mr Rickard who is standing in the doorway. The whole frontage seems to have been decorated, possibly for a carnival, although it may simply be a case of 'brightening up the home'! At this time the building on the far right was a private house, note the railings. It is now the main Post Office.

Left: THE COOMBS FAMILY, MILBORNE PORT c. 1885. This early photograph by Chaffin & Sons of Sherborne shows the young Coombs children, left to right: William (1876-1952), Florence Mary (1883-1977), Tom (1878-1964). Their parents were the village bakers and millers, George and Annie Coombs. William and Tom started their separate businesses in the early 1900s in Sherborne (see page 22) and Milborne Port respectively.

Below: PARROTT AND TADGELL, MILBORNE PORT c. 1950. Standing outside the Sansome's Hill garage is Ken Tadgell with friends. He did cycle and motor cycle repairs at the garage, formerly the Old Forge (see page 48), left to right: Roy Shepherd, -?-, Ken Swain, Maurice Grey, Ken Tadgell.

TOM COOMBS' BAKERY, MILBORNE PORT c. 1920. Tom Coombs (1878-1964) is seen here, second from left, with his workforce during a typical working day. The background ovens were wood-burning. In later years, gas ovens were installed and the bakehouse enlarged. Tom Coombs' van visited many local markets. There was also a branch of the shop in Middle Street, Yeovil from 1932 which closed in 1988.

TOM COOMBS' BAKERY, MILBORNE PORT c. 1960. George Puckett is seen here weighing out the dough for the famous Coombs lardy cakes. Pictured third from the right is David Coombs who, along with his brother Marten, took over from their father, Tom. The Coombs family were bakers and millers in the village for over two hundred years.

THE SOUTH WESTERN DAIRIES, ACREMAN STREET, SHERBORNE. The dairies were built in 1897 by Thomas E. Vincent, owner of Vincent's Stores on the corner of Half Moon Street and Digby Road (see page 20), on land he owned at the top of the street. These two pictures are taken from a publicity leaflet produced early in this century. Milk was brought in from local farms in churns and some was processed into cream or butter and the rest was bottled. In 1958 the company was taken over by United Dairies of London (later Unigate) and it finally closed in 1971. The buildings were demolished in 1976 and Acreman Court was built on the site.

A POST-WAR AERIAL VIEW OF THE SOUTH WESTERN DAIRIES. The dairy chimney was built in 1901. At the top of the picture is 'Stanley's Living', a large house owned by the Chafy family for many years.

SOME OF THE DAIRY STAFF c. 1912. These dairy workers are, back row, left to right: -?-, W. Patten, H. Axe, J. Humphreys, B. Biss, E. Davis, H. Hutchings, B. Woods, E. Biss, J. Maidment, H. Loader. Front row: E. Derrick, G. Grant, A. Ball, H. Sims, S. Dyke.

Left: TED MILLER, MILBORNE WICK c. 1973. Seen here, well after his retirement, is Ted Miller, completing a piece of dry stone walling, one of many local rural crafts. Ted worked for the Sprake family who moved to Bradley Head Farm, Milborne Wick from Minterne Magna in 1937.

Below: HAYMAKING AT BRADLEY HEAD FARM, MILBORNE WICK c. 1940. Haymaking in the 1940s was taken at a slower pace than it is using today's modern machinery. The horses, thought to be named Violet and Sergeant, wait patiently as the hay is loaded on to the rick from the cart. Working on the hayrick, left to right, are: Fred Sprake, -?-, Ted Miller (carter), Henry Sprake.

SHERBORNE CASTLE ESTATE, 1938. Until the 1940s, Percheron Grey horses were used extensively on the estate for all haulage purposes. A team of eight was kept in stables and, if necessary, all eight could be harnessed together for really heavy work.

SHERBORNE CASTLE ESTATES 1938. This team is hauling away felled trees from Purlieu. New Road and the Slopes are in the background. These horses were named with titles such as Duke, Prince or Count and others with military ranks; Admiral, Lieutenant, Sergeant. Here is Fred Northam with Duke in the lead and Prince at the rear.

MR HAROLD CLARKE, MILBORNE PORT c. 1947. Harold Clarke, proprietor of the garage, is seen, hammer in hand, doing repairs to an Austin 7. Mr Clarke also had a cycle shop in the High Street and opened the garage in Crackmore in c. 1931. Part of the original building incorporated an old polo hut that was on the site, removed from a field in Oborne.

CRACKMORE, MILBORNE PORT c. 1955. Looking down through this fine avenue of horse chestnut trees can be seen, on the right, Mr Harold Clarke's garage with a Morris car (used for taxi work) on the forecourt. Below the garage can be seen the new bus shelter built in 1954, at a cost of £118, with money provided by the Women's Institute who, in 1953, decided to mark both their twenty-first birthday and the Coronation Year in this way.

SEAGER'S GARAGE, COLDHARBOUR, SHERBORNE, EARLY 1930s. This company ran a fleet of charabancs which were in great demand for outings, as well as day trips organised by themselves, to places of interest such as Weymouth, West Bay and Cheddar Caves. Here is Mr Bill Pike, for several years the senior mechanic and fitter, who was responsible for maintaining the fleet in good running order. The business eventually became The Bere Regis Bus Company, but the garage site was demolished in the late 1980s to make way for the car park which now connects with Newland. However, the original office building remains and is now 'Scholars' restaurant.

CHILDS' GARAGE, LONG STREET, SHERBORNE c. 1935. Mr Harold Childs stands in front of the garage he built in the 1930s after moving from the cycle shop farther along the road. In the middle of the group is his brother, Ted. This business remained in the ownership of the Childs family until the 1970s, but in 1995 it closed and is awaiting demolition to make way for a housing development.

THE ABBEY BOOKSHOP, CHEAP
STREET, SHERBORNE IN THE 1920s.
Printers, as well as booksellers, occupied
this site from the time James Ellis took
over the building in the middle of the
nineteenth century. He was followed
by Joseph Sawtell, who in turn, was
succeeded by Frederick Bennett at the
turn of the century. In 1987 the last
printer left the premises and located
elsewhere in the town, but the
bookshop survives.

ROBERT ADAMS

WATCHMAKER, JEWELLER,
SILVERSMITH and OPTICIAN,

Cheap Street, Sherborne.

NOVELTIES IN

Jewellery, Souvenir Spoons,
etc., etc.

ESTABLISHED 1856.

REPAIRS PROMPTLY EXECUTED

OPPOSITE THE POST OFFICE.

Cut Flowers Supplied. Bouquets and Wreaths made to order.

8

CHEAP STREET, SHERBORNE. When Robert
Adams' shop was demolished in 1891, he moved
to new premises in Cheap Street. This picture from
Mate's Directory of 1903 shows his new shop which
is now occupied by Bath Travel Ltd. 'Opposite the
Post Office' now seems misleading, but at the time
the post office was in what is now Constance Wood
Ladieswear, where incidentally, the original post
office counter exists to this day.

Four

Schools

THE DINING HALL, WILLINGDON COLLEGE, MILBORNE PORT c. 1939.

Willingdon College

FOUNDED 1874

Milborne Porte

Somerset

Principal :
L. J. COTTINGHAM, F.C.I.S., F.F.T.COM., F.C.I.

Vice-Principal :
J. RUSSELL ORR, O.B.E., M.A.,(OXON).

Assisted by a Staff of University Graduates.
Two Qualified Matrons.

Gymnasium.

Above: THE COVER OF A BROCHURE PRODUCED BY WILLINGDON COLLEGE c. 1939. This school moved from Sussex to Ven House for the duration of the Second World War. It was a boys' boarding school with accommodation for 100 pupils, one or two of whom were local boys. The brochure says of Somerset, 'It is situated in the heart of the country, and in a district far removed from military objectives and congested areas, and at the same time readily accessible by direct line from Waterloo'.

Left: THE GYMNASIUM, WILLINGDON COLLEGE, MILBORNE PORT c. 1939. Physical education and hobbies were well catered for as this picture of the school gymnasium shows. Many popular pastimes were enjoyed such as building model aircraft and battleships, photography, woodwork and gardening. Enough was going on to keep the boys busy and take their minds off the war.

Right: WILLINGDON COLLEGE, MILBORNE PORT c. 1939. A beautiful and unusual view of Ven House from beside the little waterfall, looking towards what was at this time the rear of the house, but had once been the front. The river runs underneath the terrace on the south side of the house. The war-time safety of the pupils was ensured by air-raid shelters in the large underground, fireproof vaults which accommodated 150 people.

Below: A CLASSROOM, WILLINGDON COLLEGE, MILBORNE PORT c. 1939. Many of the fine rooms at Ven House were used as classrooms, the school being divided into junior and senior sections. The fees were 25 guineas (£26.25) per term for boys aged six to nine years, 30 guineas (£31.50) for boys aged ten to thirteen years and 35 guineas (£36.75) for boys over the age of thirteen years. Private piano lessons were given by Mr H. Sinclair, the local church organist, at a cost of £2 12s 6d (£2.63) per term. It 'was hoped that after passing their School Certificates, the boys would go on to take the Higher School Certificate and then enter from college direct to university'.

SHERBORNE SCHOOL. Locally known as The King's School, this famous public school for boys, was refounded in 1550 as The Free Grammar School of King Edward VI (hence 'King's' School). It was transformed into its present status by H.D. Harper, the headmaster, seen here in 1877 with some of the senior boys.

THE FORMER SWIMMING BATH OF SHERBORNE SCHOOL. In 1866 Harper had proposed to the school governors that a properly equipped swimming pool should be provided, but it was not until 1873 that the bath was completed. At first it was fed by the Coombe and Newell streams and, says A.B. Gourlay in his History of Sherborne School, 'the boys often bathed in what looked like café au lait'! The sides and floor were not concreted over until 1909. It was closed in 1976 when the new sports centre was opened and the site is now occupied by the school works department.

SHERBORNE SCHOOL FOR GIRLS. The girls' school was built in Bradford Road in 1903 and before that date was accommodated in Ramsam House on Greenhill (now Collegiate House). A clock tower was added (at the right hand side of this picture) in 1926. The school was founded by the efforts of Mrs Kenelm Wingfield Digby in 1899 and Miss Mulliner was the first headmistress.

THE WHOLE SCHOOL IN 1905. According to the museum's records, six years before this there had only been fourteen pupils, six of whom were boys, so some idea may be gained of the school's rapid growth. The buildings shown here are also in Bradford Road, but to the west of those in the picture above.

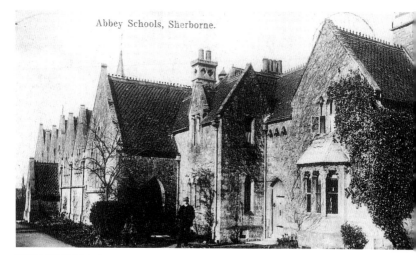

THE ABBEY PRIMARY SCHOOL, HORSECASTLES, SHERBORNE. This school was built in 1855 to accommodate some 600 pupils from the town and nearby villages. Originally it was divided into three departments, boys, girls and infants, each with its own head teacher and staff. This is an early twentieth-century postcard, believed to show Mr W.J. Ingram who was headmaster from 1876 to 1919.

AN ABBEY SCHOOL GIRLS' CLASS OF 1923-4. Pupils in the photograph are, back row, left to right: R. Curtis, D. Mitchell, ? Houghton, C. Andrews, E. Southey. Middle row: -?-, Miss Martin (headmistress), J. Hann, E. Luffman, E. Clark, J. Martin, Miss Abbott (student teacher), E. Bide. Front row: E. Noake, G. Huss, L. Meade, E. Finch, D. Roberts.

THE CHURCH SCHOOL, MILBORNE PORT c. 1930. The school was opened on this site in 1864 and was known as the National School (see page 47) and finally closed on 20 July 1979. It was built to a very high standard by Mr A. Reynolds for Sir W.C. Medlycott. Here is Group III with their teacher, standing, left to right: Yvonne Andrews, Richard Gosney, Rowland Luffman, Lilian Chant, -?-, Miss Maidment (teacher), Mary King, Winnie Summers, Kathy Batten, Lily Dungey. Front row: Lionel Parsons, Albert Mitchell, Ken Riggs, Bert Parsons, Betty Griffin, ? Haggett. Second row: Hugh Scammell, Fred Perry, Ronald Downton, Roy Hallett, Joan Dyer, Ruby Barter. Third row: -?-, Cicely Cabell, the Rolls brothers. Fourth row: Arthur Scammell, O. Bull, Edith Pullen, Nancy Day.

THE CHURCH SCHOOL, MILBORNE PORT c. 1935. Group IV with their teacher in what may be a reading lesson because on their desks are the comics of the day! Back row, left to right: Muriel Puckett, Tom Smith, Muriel Davis, Donald Leach, Mrs Pilkington (teacher), Douglas Cabell, Agnes Cook, Mary Lovelace, Jack Riggs. Third row: Jean King, John Raymond, Lily Trivett, Ronald Hallett, Linda Rolls, John Hogarth, Grace Burrows, Gordon Crabb. Second row: Audrey Jackson, Kenneth Dyke, Eileen Critchell, Doreen Cornick, Iris Cabell, Joyce Cooper, Sybil Downton, Joyce Hallett. Standing, behind front row: Doris Lamb, -?-, Sheila Fox, Royce Griffen. Front row: Desmond Curtis, Betty Winter, George Dyer, Kelson Rown, Joan Mitchell, William Bull, Dick Luffman.

FOSTER'S SCHOOL, SHERBORNE c. 1900. Founded in 1640 by Richard Foster, Yeoman, it was accommodated in various buildings in the town, until it moved to a purpose built schoolroom, seen here on the left, in 1875. At this time there were forty pupils, although according to the Western Gazette of 19 April 1875, 'others were applying for admission'. The headmaster's residence and boarding house were built by George Pitman of Milborne Port and were occupied in February 1887. As schoolroom and boarding house, the buildings remained in use until October 1939 when the new school in Tinneys Lane was completed, but the boarding house was occupied until 1986. The buildings then remained empty and boarded up until Dorset County Council sold them in 1995. At the time of writing the site is being developed into seven houses and three apartments.

FOSTER'S SCHOOL IN TINNEYS LANE. Built in 1939 by Mr E.G. Wilkins of Marnhull at a cost of £21,000, the school was enlarged after the Second World War by extending the eastern end of the building and later by the addition of a number of 'temporary' classrooms which remained in use until the school was demolished in September 1994 when the new Gryphon Comprehensive School opened on the old St Aldhelm's school site.

SHERBORNE HOUSE IN NEWLAND. The house was occupied from 1931 to 1992 by Lord Digby's School for Girls. Strictly speaking, this photograph is not of Lord Digby's School as it was taken very early in the twentieth century. Built in the eighteenth century for the Portman family, it is also remembered as the home from 1850 to 1860 of William Charles Macready, the great actor-manager. The Thornhill murals on the walls and ceiling of the main staircase remain to this day. The school closed in 1992 when the Gryphon School opened although the building was used by that school for another two years until its new buildings were ready.

LORD DIGBY'S SCHOOL 1917. Miss Churchill, assistant mistress, with her form. At this time the school was accommodated in a Regency house opposite Sherborne House in Newland, approximately where a Somerfield Supermarket now stands. It was during this year that Miss Margaret Billinger was appointed headmistress, a post she held until her death in 1942. At the time she was appointed, there were sixty six girls at the school. Miss Churchill was the only other teacher apart from a pupil teacher who was paid three shillings (15p) a week!

FOSTER'S INFANTS' SCHOOL, SHERBORNE 1911. This school building was in Newland at the end of Tinneys Lane. It was bombed in September 1940 and totally demolished but fortunately the children had all left for the day. After the war Newland Flats were built on the site. This picture shows the headmistress, Miss Pursey, with those pupils who had achieved 100% attendance in the 1910-11 school year.

CLASS I OF FOSTER'S INFANTS' SCHOOL IN 1932. It is interesting to see that although the class size appears to be only thirty pupils, the classroom obviously was designed to hold twice as many. Note the gas lighting. Although the children have not all been identified, the following are known to be in the picture: M. Cleal, M. Richards, J. Rolls, B. Ryde and E. Phillips.

LORD DIGBY'S SCHOOL INFANTS, SHERBORNE c. 1900. Lord Digby's School had an infants class at this time, held in Macready House next door to Sherborne House. In 1835 this building was called the Sherborne Mechanics' Institute and after 1850 the Sherborne Literary Institute. From the 1940s until the 80s it was used by the Sherborne Youth Club until the club moved to the purpose built Youth Centre in Tinneys Lane. These two pictures show the staff; Miss Taylor, Miss Sampson and Miss Ruegg and pupils, including; Douglas Stewart, Eddie and Lilian Peskett, Hilda Lowman, Joyce Dyer and Freda Cowling.

THE COUNCIL SCHOOL, MILBORNE PORT c. 1932. This was one of the two main schools in Milborne Port, the other being the church school. The new school building was opened on 11 April 1912, the school having moved from the old schoolrooms in the Congregational church (the British School). On the right hand side, left to right, are: Alan Brooke, George Barrett, Arther Brooke, Herbert Barrett, Ted Smith. Front row: Vic Penny, Dave Cabell, -?-. Second row: Tom Jackson, Tom Ham, Dave Jackson, Tony Buckley. Third row: Pat Papworth, Hugh Chant, Fred Pearce, Ted Hall. Fourth row: Lionel Brooke, Bill Parsons, Tony Hansford, -?-. Back row: Jack Hann, Ted Penny, John Morecombe, Bill Myall. Standing at rear: Mr F. Matthews (teacher).

THE COUNCIL SCHOOL, MILBORNE PORT 1955. This later picture dated 19 July shows the top class with their teacher. Top row, left to right: Richard Hann, David Painter, Keith Moorse, Michael Hann, Billy Dungey, Keith Lee, Mr R. Beckett (teacher), Raymond Woodley, Michael Brace, Kathleen Judd, Pat Axe, Christine Clothier. Middle row: Joan Merritt, Suzette Durrant, Josephine Weller, John Broom, Sheila Cooper, Jennifer Raymond, Sheena Hewlett, Suzanne Ackland, Colin Hindmarsh, Terry Davis. Front row: Heather Caines, Christine Cuss, Jean Candy, Jean Higgins, Brenda Kelso, June Hinks, Carol Trott, Susan Parsons, Steven Moorse, John Harvey, Richard Duckworth, David Burge.

THE COUNCIL SCHOOL, SIMONS ROAD, SHERBORNE. Built in 1912, this school took its first pupils in July 1913. This picture of Class III is probably from about 1916.

THE COUNCIL SCHOOL, SHERBORNE 1930. Could the '5' have been the class number? In the picture are, back row, left to right: Jack Woods, Reg Keech, 'Bronco' Bowditch, Jim Wild, ? Diment, Ernest Howard, -?-, George Ashton, John Watts. Middle row: Doug Irvine, ? Guppy, Daisy Shepherd, Ruth Reeves, Norah Biss, ? Biss, Phyllis Andrews, Rose Hatcher, Cyril Good, Cyril Curtis. Front row: R. Hamblin, Doug Kendall, J. Eveleigh, Bill Ryde, Phyllis Lazenbury, Vera Andrews, Betty Richards, -?-, Roy Cranton, Ted Chant, Peter Gear, Ron Thorn.

THE LONG STREET SCHOOL, SHERBORNE. The schoolroom was added to the Congregational church in 1852. Here, in about 1900, are some of the pupils with the head teacher, Mr John Pooley.

THE LONG STREET SCHOOLROOM, SHERBORNE. The schoolroom is decorated for a Harvest Festival just before the First World War. From the rail, wall to wall curtains were hung to separate the classes. Note the fish-tail gas lighting.

Five

Music, Fun and Games

THE AMATEUR PLAYERS OF SHERBORNE. The company was formed in 1934 by Fred Alcock. Here he is in Dear Brutus with his daughter, Joy, in 1946.

THE AMATEUR PLAYERS OF SHERBORNE 1935. The company performed No, No, Nanette to packed houses in the Carlton Theatre. Here in a still from it are Jack Perham, Joan Waller, Betty Shaw, Eileen Wright, Beryl Heath, Peggy Henstridge and Beryl Chaffin.

THE AMATEUR PLAYERS OF SHERBORNE 1967. This production was Free as Air, and the cast included Bill Pike, Stanley McKay, Meg Whittingdale, Hester Jesson, Roger Burridge, and John Riley, all of whom are in this scene.

MILBORNE PORT AMATEUR DRAMATIC SOCIETY 1951. In 1946 the local WI started an Amateur Dramatic Section which eventually became the Amateur Dramatic Society. They put on many shows in the old Victoria Hall and, considering the size of the stage, managed to create some marvellous sets. This is the cast of The Happiest Days of Your Life, produced in 1951, back row, left to right: T. Davis, Mrs Hyde, Mrs A. Southcombe, David Hallett, Avril Stanier, Alan Hindmarsh, Mrs Craggs, Reg Raymond, Mr Williams, David Davis, Frank Wooley, Mrs Peake, Hector Southcombe. Kneeling: Lydia Craggs, Sheila Hann, Norman King.

MILBORNE PORT TOC H c. 1955. This Toc H concert party are probably entertaining at the old people's party in the Victoria Hall in North Street. Back row, left to right: T. Dyke, -?-, K. Beard, S. Mitchell, S. Dycer, Revd E.D. Buxton, A Peake, -?-, G. Jackson. Front row: R. Lacey, Jock Parker, W. Topp, G. Heritage.

SHERBORNE TOWN BAND 1907. The band was formed in 1906 by Mr S. Beaton from some members of his old military band, which had existed in the 1880s and '90s and also from the old 'Volunteer Band' of the time. Back row, left to right: H. Bown, W. Ring, ? Cridge, A. Plympton, G. Hamblin, H. Maber. Second row: C. Crocker, E. Curtis, A. Tulk, W. Russell (later bandmaster), T. Wakeling, W. Gander, T. Gillard, G. Read, C. Williamson. Third row: H. Newport, T. Monkton, A. Day, S. Beaton (bandmaster), T. Parsons, J. Coombs, F. Sugg, A. Lowman. Seated: -?-, G. Lowman, J. Elliott, A. Parsons, F. Crocker.

THE SALVATION ARMY BAND, SHERBORNE IN THE 1920s. Standing, left to right: B. Cable, J. Seal, E. Dawson, Captain Phillips, D. Redfern, -?-. Seated: -?-, G. Noake, A. Northam, B. Richards, B. Weake, -?-. Front row: ? Hann, M. Pest, V. Sansom, A. Wells. Every Saturday evening this band played on the corner of Upper Cheap Street and The Green.

Right: MILBORNE PORT BOYS' BRIGADE
BAND c. 1954. For many years church parades
were quite large occasions for all the local
youth organisations and were always led by the
Boys' Brigade Band. The route was determined
by which church was the final destination and
took approximately thirty minutes.
The band here is going along the High Street
led by mace carrier Fred Coombes. The three
side-drummers are, left to right: John King, -?-,
Maurice Hiscock.

Below: MILBORNE PORT TOWN BAND.
Most likely this performance took place during
a fete at Ven House in 1896 or '97. The
fourteen band members are pictured here with
their bandmaster, Mr H.J. Pitman, holding the
baton. Records show that a band existed in the
village in the early 1800s.

SHERBORNE CARNIVAL 1907. Carnivals were held nearly every year. Up to 1939 they were organised by the 'Bonfire Boys' committee. Here is Bradford & Sons' entry standing in their yard. The railway and the Slopes are in the background.

A SHERBORNE CARNIVAL ENTRY OF THE 1930s. This one has been entered by the Sports Club. Among those identified in this picture are Jack Wiltshire, Reg Gregory, Eddie Russell and Miss Freeman.

MILBORNE PORT BOYS' BRIGADE JUBILEE CELEBRATIONS 1953. A large group of members took part, past and present and from both local and other companies of the Wessex Battalion Boys' Brigade, paraded through the village on 3 May 1953. The parade, to celebrate the company's silver jubilee, was led by the band of the 1st Sherborne Company with additional members drawn from other companies. The Old Boys, seen here in Coldharbour, were waiting to enter the Methodist church. During the service a presentation was made to Captain Rosewarne Dyke and his cousin, Lieutenant T.E. Dyke for fifty years' loyal service with the company.

FANCY DRESS PARADE, MILBORNE PORT c. 1960. Coldharbour was often the assembly point for fancy dress parades that then went on to the local fete. The parade, usually led by the Boys' Brigade band would proceed to Ven Gardens, or in later years, to the Memorial Playing Fields. On the left of the picture is Marion Farnes with her daughter Lesley, Stuart Hinks and Mrs Hallett. The Oxo girl is Jacqueline Ackland and the cowboy, Bernard Ackland. On the extreme right is Janet Stone. Standing on the trailer, third from left is Julia Mollon and fourth from left, Joy Moorse.

THE HOSPITAL SHIP, 'YEATMAN'. This is an entry in the 1930 Sherborne Carnival. This magnificent float is parading in South Street.

THE CHURCH LADS' BRIGADE FLOAT, SHERBORNE CARNIVAL IN THE 1920s. This float is mounted on a lorry belonging to the Cow & Gate Company in South Street.

FRED DOWNTON OF MILBORNE PORT IN 1953. Undoubtedly one of the great characters of the village was Fred Downton. Always at the centre of any fun or laughter, he had a wonderful sense of humour and invariably took part in any fete or fancy dress parade. Here he is at the Coronation Fete on 2 June 1953, dressed as John Peel, with many amused villagers looking on.

MILBORNE PORT FLOWER SHOW 1913. This was possibly the last show or fete to be held until after the Great War and was probably held in Barley Close behind Ven House. This old postcard was one of many issued to mark this event, and together with the others, it tells us that it was a 'large Show with a Fancy Dress Competition and Sports for the Children'. It shows the fashions of the day well too.

THE CHURCH LADS' BRIGADE OUTSIDE SHERBORNE ABBEY IN 1932. Back row, left to right: ? Norris, A. Mead, ? Marsh, ? Lacey, H. Shepherd, D. Biss, J. Biss, G. Back, R. Wiscombe, E. Park, ? Bishop, G. Jones, A. Martin, V. Ford. Third row: A. Jones, W. Ford, H. Holmes, A. Gourlay, S. Thompson, S. Hey, D. Ballam, G. Biss, J. Stone, N. Baker, ? Edwards. Second row: -?-, F. Mead, W. Henning, G. Brett, G. Ford, Revd M. Askwith, F. Morris, Revd A. Field, ? Smith, ? Marsh. Seated: ? Ball, G. Ashton, ? Martin, ? Osborne, ? Lush, M. Dowse, E. Henstridge, ? Wiscombe, S. Pullen. Inset: L. Perry, Miss Rawson, ? Trask, S. Guppy.

THE BOYS' BRIGADE, SHERBORNE. Before the Second World War, the town always had a strong contingent of the brigade. In 1942 it celebrated its fiftieth anniversary, and at about this time, amalgamated with the town's Church Lads' Brigade to form one organisation. Here they are in the gymnasium of the King's School which is now part of the dining complex.

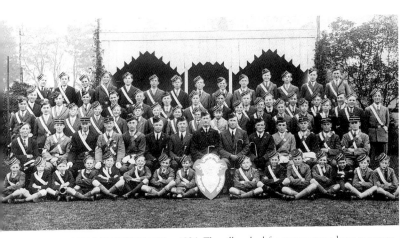

MILBORNE PORT BOYS' BRIGADE c. 1926. The village had for many years a large company of the Boy's Brigade formed in 1905. Sadly, the brigade was disbanded with the closing of the Methodist church in July 1988. This picture shows the company in 1926 with their captain, H.R. Dyke, and displaying the Lucas Tooth Drill Shield they had won.

MILBORNE PORT CHURCH LADS' BRIGADE c.1911. This scene was possibly photographed close to the old church school as the boys, and one girl, are seen with their leader, Captain R.W. Dickinson, who was also the headmaster of the school at the time. Back row, left to right: A. Grinter, F. Rown, E. Chant, A. Andrews, W. Grinter, G. Cubitt, J. Gosney. Seated: G. Raymond, B. Tizzard, Dolly Dickinson, Captain R.W. Dickinson, F. Shepherd, F. Walters, A. Walters. Front row: T. Fudge, B. Hann, D. Luffman, H. King.

MILBORNE PORT RED CROSS c. 1946. This group is at Limerick with their ambulance which had been built and put on the road by voluntary subscription. It was used not only in the village, but in the surrounding villages as well. Back row, left to right: Mr Hopkins, Mrs Luffman, -?-, Mr H. Gully, Mr Penny, Mr Hannam, Mrs Pullen. Middle row: Mrs Mitchell, Mrs Brooks, Mrs Jennings, Hon. Mrs Bramwell, Mrs K. Cory, Mrs P. Trott. Front row: Mrs S. Hallett, Mrs E. Hinks, Miss M. Wilkins.

MILBORNE PORT WOMENS' INSTITUTE 1953. The WI have been in existence in the village since 1932 and now have their own centre in the Town Hall. During the last sixty years they have been involved in many projects to help the village. During the Second World War they carried out many fund-raising events and also helped with the first child evacuees. In 1938 great jam-making sessions were under way, as the WI could buy sugar cheaply at 37s 6d (£1.85) a hundredweight, but members protested at the high salaries and expenses paid to the official examiners of the jam they produced. Here celebrating their twenty first anniversary and the Queen's Coronation are, back row, left to right: Mrs Curtis, Mrs B. Davis, Mrs Ashford, Mrs B. Rendell, Mrs Raymond, Miss R. Harris, Mrs Pullen, Mrs D. Spiller, -?-. Front row: Mrs Pitman, Mrs Wilkins, Mrs Cory, Mrs H. Southcombe, Mrs Earle, Mrs Miller, Mrs Hyde, Mrs Smart.

THE MILBORNE PORT PLATOON OF THE HOME GUARD. Milborne Port's Dad's Army at Limerick on 3 December 1944 just before the Home Guard stood down. Top row, left to right: L/Cpl G. Batten, Ptes R. Button, E. Dungey, J. Crossley, A. Mitchell, E. Masters, B. Guppy, H. Mitchell, W. Biddiscombe, L/Cpl D. King. Second row: L/Cpl P. Durrant, Ptes A. Hannam, S. Dowding, L. West, L. Raison, J. Waltham, T. Hallett, A. Brown, L/Cpl A. Higgins, Pte H. Scammell. Third row: L/Cpl C.W. Weller, Pte H. Thompson, L/Cpl E. Frost, L/Cpl C. Tuck, Ptes L. Grimes, R. Waltham, P. Hallett, R. Marsh, F. Stanier, W. Hinde. Fourth row: Cpls G. Heritage, A. Davis, H. Smith, Sgt A. Snook, Capt. H. Southcombe, Major B.B. Dyke, Lieut. J.E.T. Buck, 2nd Lt F.W. Rown, Sgts G. Lamb, B. Ham, Cpls P. Durrant, H. Cabell. Sitting, front: Ptes S. White, R. Lewis, A. Chant, L/Cpl C.L. Lane, Ptes W. Cooper, B. Cook.

MR AND MRS HECTOR SOUTHCOMBE'S SILVER WEDDING CELEBRATION, MILBORNE PORT, 1955. A large gathering of family, friends and workers from the Thomas Ensor Glove factory assembled in the factory grounds for this anniversary. Front row, left to right: Mr S. Southcombe, Mrs E. Southcombe, Mr R. Southcombe, Mrs Q. Coles, Mrs B. Southcombe, Mr H. Southcombe, Mrs A. Southcombe, Mr D. Southcombe, -?-, Miss M. Clark, -?-, Mr J. Clark, Snr, Mrs M. Clark, Mrs O. Clark, Mr J. Clark, Jnr.

MILBORNE PORT PARISH CHURCH SUNDAY SCHOOL 1958. The cast of the Sunday school nativity play posing on the stage of the Church House. Back row, left to right: Susan Parsons, Ann Dryden, Susan Gully, Norman Jackson, Mrs Helen Coombs (teacher), Mr Dick Hammond (Father Christmas), Heather Caines, Elizabeth Rendell, Jennifer Legg-Bagg, Viv Fox. Front row: Julia Mollon, Anita Coombs, Lucy Buxton, Audrey Pullen, Judith Butcher, Noel Parsons, Mary Buxton, Sarah Duckworth.

MILBORNE PORT BRITISH LEGION QUIZ TEAMS c. 1952. The victorious ladies' team is seen receiving the cup from Mrs P. Gear at the Slessor Club in Sherborne. The team had just outwitted the men's team in the final. Seen here looking on at the presentation are, left to right: Mr S. McKay, Mr T. Dyke, Dr N. Rhys-Davies, Mrs S. Southcombe, Mrs P. Gear, Mr D. Mildenhall (quizmaster), Mrs Q. Coles, Mrs C. Southcombe, Mrs F. Luffman, Mrs A. Southcombe.

MILBORNE PORT CHILD WELFARE CLINIC PARTY c. 1950. A wonderful looking group of mothers and children at the Christmas Party in the Church House. Many of these babies will now be parents themselves. The clinic met regularly in the Church House to weigh the children and issue cod liver oil and orange juice. The mothers and children here are with; Mrs P. Trott (centre, in uniform), Mrs A. Southcombe, Mrs D. Spiller, Nurse Marshall, Mrs Topp, Mrs Tuck.

2nd MILBORNE PORT GIRL GUIDES 1954. The 1st Milborne Port Company was formed in 1925 by Miss H. Shingleton who was captain until 1929. The company closed in 1934. On 10 June 1942, the company was reformed under the captaincy of Mrs G. Holbrook and in 1952 it was re-registered as the 2nd Milborne Port Company, possibly because it was no longer linked to the church. Seen here in 1954 are the Guides and Rangers with captain, Miss B. Coakes. Back row, left to right: Pam Dite, Bridget Hiscock, Rosemary Rendall, Joyce Hodges, Christine Clothier, Karen Hinks, Pam Kingsbury, Josephine Weller. Middle row: Mary Dycer, Ruth Pidgeon, Shirley Fudge, Rita Skinner, Gillian Dite, Ann Viner, Diane Williams, Edna Luffman, Mary Cuss, Irene Davies. Front row: Kathleen Hopkins, Cynthia Bowden, Pat Smith, Brenda Kelso, Beryl Coakes, Muriel Puckett, Geoffrey Murrells, Kathleen Judd.

SHERBORNE FOOTBALL CLUB 1921-22. Winners of the Shaftesbury and District League and the Dorset Junior League Northern Section. Back row, left to right: H. Hindle (chairman), C. Caines, S. Hunt, R. Heathman, C. Wilson, C. White, R. Kennell (linesman). Seated: W. Tebbitt (treasurer), A. Hatt (hon.secretary), S. Cuff, G. Ewens, H. Ireland (captain), B. Norris, E. Curtis, R. Gibling, F. Vosper (chairman). On ground: A. Muskett, W. Sims.

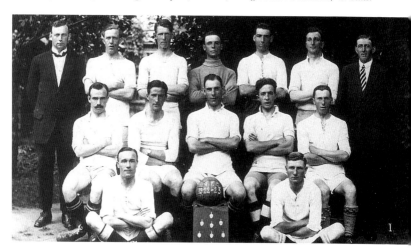

SHERBORNE FOOTBALL CLUB 1922-23. This team were finalists in the Shaftesbury Charity Cup. Back row, left to right: F. Vosper (chairman), S. Hunt, P. Bown, R. Heathman, C. Caines, E. Oxford, W. Sims (linesman). Seated: A. Hatt, G. Ewens (vice-captain), H. Ireland (captain), B. Norris, S. Cuff. On ground: A. Muskett, B. Wiscombe.

MILBORNE PORT FOOTBALL CLUB, 1st XI 1951-52. The football club was established in the village in 1891 after the glove factories adopted a five and a half day week. After a public meeting, Mr H. Blandford proposed that organised football should be played so that the young men could dispose of their excess energy! Pictured here in 1951 is the team photograph taken at the Jubilee Field in Goathill Road. The pavilion in the background was made from old aircraft packing crates. Back row, left to right: P. Durrant (hon. secretary), F. Downton (groundsman), T. Smith, G. Webber, S. Hinks, B. Guppy, D. Stacey, L. Barter, J. Durrant, G. Steele. Front row: R. Craggs, G. Oatley, W. Kelso, A. Hannam, D. Budd.

MILBORNE PORT FOOTBALL CLUB 1967-68. At the Memorial Playing Fields are the combined teams with the cups they had won during that season, which were: The Blackmore Vale Charity Cup, The Merthyr Guest Cup, The McCreery Cup, The John Hayward and Yeovil & District Under-17 Cups. The Reserve Team were also runners-up in Division Three of the Yeovil League. Front row, left to right: F. Fortino, D. Creighton, G. Knight, J. Henshaw, L. Arnold, W. Hughes. Second row, seated: J. Newman, G. Webber, G. Myall, P. Miller, R. Harvey (captain), K. Moorse. Third row: F. Hillier (chairman), R. Farnes, T. Cook, ? Rendall, R. Creighton, R. Morgan, ? Button, F. Whitmore, P. Davis, R. Biss (vice-captain), B. Fenn, D. Cook, S. Davis, C. Warren, S. Hinks, N. Hinks, F. Coombes. Back row: R. Halson, K. Loader, P. Dodds, P. Pitman, M. Biss.

SHERBORNE CRICKET CLUB 1900. The team is seen outside the old pavilion on the Terrace. The following have been identified, standing: third from left, Mr Ford; third from right, Tom Bowley. Seated: first from right, H. Seymour (Town Clerk).

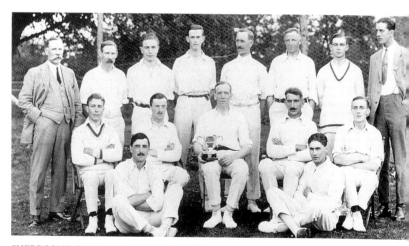

SHERBORNE CRICKET CLUB IN THE 1920s. Standing, left to right: E. Hill (umpire), A. Baker, E. Davidge, A. Coombs, D. Brown, Canon S.H. Wingfield, ? Digby, E. Paine, C. Bow (scorer). Seated: P. Davidge, E. Maidment, F. Trevett (captain), F. Cooke, W. Russell. On ground: R. Ponsford, R. Muss.

MILBORNE PORT SOCIAL CRICKET CLUB 1928. Milborne Port had two men's cricket clubs for many years, one of which is shown here at Mr T. Dyke's Cheriton grass tennis courts. The team played on a field near Newtown belonging to Mr H. Hallett. Back row, left to right: H. Hamblin (umpire), C. Gibbs, F. Parsons, G. King (vice-captain), W. Warren, C. Luffman, E. Frost, W. Harvey, T. Perkins. Front row, seated: E. Penny (hon. secretary), A. Davis, P. Hopkins, W. Hyde (captain), J. Spiller, B. Snook, A. Luffman, F. King, J. Pullen.

MILBORNE PORT CRICKET CLUB 1959. Records show that the cricket club is the oldest sporting organisation in the village, having started in the early part of the 1800s. For many years the club played on a pitch at Station Road, close to the site of the present day pitch. The team here standing on the pavilion steps at Morlands, Glastonbury is, left to right: Dr N. Rhys-Davies, B. Webber, C. Hinks, F. Shepherd (umpire), -?-, L. Parsons, L. Harvey, F. Pearce, A. Clepitt, P. Harvey, L. Barter, A. Abbott (scorer), M. Moorse.

SHERBORNE HOCKEY CLUB 1949. The ladies' hockey team in 1949 consisted of, back row, left to right: -?-, A. Lush, M. Hellyar, B. Mackerness. Middle row: V. Upshall, W. Ryall, N. Jowett. Front row: M. Kennell, J. Pidden, N. Linney, E. Youdle, J. Ginn.

SHERBORNE HOCKEY CLUB 1936. The mixed team of 1936 consisted of, back row: H. Hunt, J. Green, A. Allen, E. Gibbs, G. Brett, S. Guppy, K. Baker, G. Hunt. Front row: Mrs A. Allen, D. Lambert, E. Ashford, J. Sharp.

SHERBORNE LAUNDRY LADIES' FOOTBALL TEAM 1933. Back row: L. Baker, P. Andrews, M. Peaty, D. Redfern, I. Quirk. Seated: W. Roberts, F. Catchpole, V. Evans, I. Batten, D. Peaty. On ground: ? Best, M. Vincent.

MILBORNE PORT LADIES' CRICKET TEAM 1937. Between the two World Wars the village had a ladies' cricket team as well as two men's teams. The ladies used to play at Limerick and are pictured here in c. 1937. Back row, left to right: Alice Pullen, Betty Moorse, Esme Hallett, Muriel Critchell, Freda Pullen, Winnie Dungey, Wanda Cory, -?-, Mary Bull. Front row: -?-, Hazel Pullen.

Sherborne Diversions,
1831.

To be Run for, over Lenthay Course, on Wednesday, August 3,
A PURSE OF

TWENTY SOVEREIGNS,

For any Horse, Mare, or Gelding, that never won a Plate, Cup, or Sweepstakes of the value of Fifty Pounds, to carry Weight for Age as follows, viz. :—Two-years-olds, a Feather ; Three Years, 6st. 12lb. ; Four Years, 8st. ; Five Years, 8st. 7lb. ; Six Years, 9st. ; and Aged, 9st. 2lb. The best of three Heats, three times round the Course. A distance. The Winner of one Purse on this Course to carry 5lb. extra : if more than one, 7lb.—A Clear Heat for the Stakes.

Mr. Washington's	br. g.	COMUS,	4 years old,	8st. 2lb.	Red, Black Cap.
Mr. Carter's	dr. m.	ALICE GRAY,	Aged,		Purple, and Black.
Mr. Hill's	g. g.	DWARF,	Aged,	9st. 2lb.	Black, Crimson and Black Cap.
Mr. Montgomery's	b. g.	GOSHAWK,	Aged,	9st. 2lb.	Blue and Orange, Black Cap.
Mr. Hopkins's	b. m.	MISS WOLVERTON,	5 years old,	9st.	Straw Jacket, Black Cap.
Mr. Brains's		TILLEY,	Aged,	8st. 2lb.	Blue, and Scarlet.
Mr. Freke's	b. m.	No NAME,	3 years old,	6st. 12lb.	Blue, Scarlet and Black Cap.

SAME DAY,——A PURSE OF

TEN SOVEREIGNS,

For any Horse, Mare, or Gelding, not exceeding Fourteen Hands High, that never won Twenty Pounds at any one time, to carry Weight for Age and Inches. The Winner of Ten Pounds at any one time to carry 5lb. extra.—Heats, twice round the Course. A distance.—A Clear Heat for the Stakes.

Mr. Wadman's	b. m.	CREEPING JANE,	5 years old,	11 hands 2 inches,	7st. 10lb.	Red, and Black Cap.
Mr. Hill's	b. g.	PARAWHI,	4 years old,	13 hands,	8st. 6lb.	Black, Crimson and Black Cap.
Mr. Wilkins's	b. m.	AMELIA,	4 years old,	13 hands, 6st. 11lb.	Green Body and Sleeves, and Scarlet Cap.
Mr. Hopkins's	ch. m.	LITTY ANNE,	3 years old,	13 hands 2 inches,	7st. 7lb.	Straw Jacket, Black Cap.
Mr. Freke's	ch. m.	GOVERNESS,	Aged,	13 hands 2 inches,	7st. 7lb.	Blue and Scarlet, Black Cap.

AND SAME DAY

A HANDICAP PURSE OF 5 SOVEREIGNS,

For the beaten Cavalry Horses the first day.—Heats twice round the Course.—Not less than three to start.

Mr. Burrow's	b. m.	LIONESS,	5 years old,	7st. 7lb.	Scarlet, and Black Cap.
Mr. Taylor's	c.	TOMMY TACKLE,	5 years old,	7st.	Scarlet, and Black Cap.
Mr. Miller's	g. m.	ADELAIDE,	4 years old,	8st.	Pink Jacket, Black and Pink Cap.
Mr. Tucker's	b. m.	MATILDA,	4 years old,	8st.	Scarlet, and Black Cap.
Mr. Cox's	c. g.	SUBSCRIPTION,	Aged,	8st.	Pink Stripe, and Black Cap.
Sir Aurero's	b. g.	RED ROBIN,	5 years old,	7st. 7lb.	Blue, and White.

Above: SHERBORNE PARK IN JULY 1927. Mr C.J.F. Greenham organised a Donkey Derby in Sherborne Park to raise funds for the Yeatman Hospital. Many well-known jockeys took part, including Steve Donoghue, E. Elliott, E. Smith, J. Brennan, Gordon Richards, Cecil Ray, Charlie Smirke, P. Mayor, K. Gethin and J. Sirett.

Left: RACING AT SHERBORNE, AUGUST 1831. A poster advertising horse racing at Lenthay. Unfortunately Sherborne Museum has no records of the results!

Six

Local Transport

STEAM TRACTION ENGINES AT PACK MONDAY FAIR IN THE 1930s. The fair in the thirties was always held in the Old Fairfield, Coldharbour. These engines were owned by Anderton and Rowland and were named, from left to right: Lord Nelson, Lion, Dragon and Queen Mary.

MILBORNE PORT STATION 1961. On 24 June 1961, a rebuilt Pacific locomotive hurries the express through Milborne Port towards Sherborne after the climb from Templecombe. In the early part of the twentieth century, Milborne Port station was a busy place for goods traffic, having its own goods shed and station lorry. Most of the goods arriving at the station were destined for the local glove factories and other businesses. Some goods also went back out from the gloving factories. Because the station was situated one and a half miles from the village centre, passenger traffic was lighter. Milborne Port station was open from 1860 until 1966.

ARRIVING AT MILBORNE PORT STATION 1961. Also on the 24 June 1961 a Standard Class 4 No 76006 pauses to let passengers disembark from the midday stopping train from Salisbury. This train followed the express pictured above and probably completed its run at Yeovil. On the edge of the platform Fritz (John) Cory waits to pick up his passengers who were coming from Gillingham to the fete at Ven House, Milborne Port. Mr Cory's first car, a Vauxhall Wyvern, can just be seen on the right of the picture.

Right: MILBORNE PORT STATION 1937. Possibly the largest group of passengers ever seen on the platform at Milborne Port Station at any one time. They are all employees of Silas Dyke who were boarding a special train for London for their centenary outing in May 1937. Clearly seen on the left are the old oil lamps that provided dim lighting for Milborne Port station.

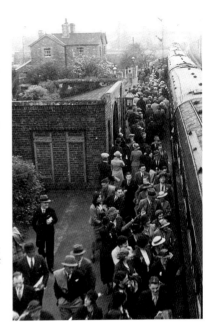

Below: A DELTIC BETWEEN SHERBORNE AND MILBORNE PORT c. 1981. A very rare visitor indeed to the old Southern Region. This Deltic 9016, Gordon Highlander, speeds its special train towards the site of the old Milborne Port Station after a steep 1 in 80 climb from Sherborne. The Deltics, for many years, ran on the East Coast main line from Kings Cross to Scotland and hauled the Flying Scotsman. To many they were one of the finest diesel locomotives ever made. Just seen in the background, Three Arch Bridge, set at the top of Sherborne Bank, was the Mecca of many small boys, and their fathers, in the days of steam trains.

STICKLAND'S VAN, SHERBORNE. On this and the next page are the vehicles owned by four local businesses. Firstly, standing in front of this 1920s van owned by Sticklands is Mr Insole who partnered Mr Rolls and Mr Hunt in running the business after Mr Stickland died. They also had a shop in Milborne Port for a time.

THE SHERBORNE LAUNDRY c. 1935. The laundry had a small fleet of vehicles for collection and delivery. The drivers and their assistants in this picture are, from left to right: D. Vickery, R. Lane, H. Hunt, J. Chubb, L. Crane, S. Vickery.

THE SOUTH WESTERN DAIRIES, SHERBORNE. Unloading a lorry in the 1960s.
Mr A. Peach is on the left of the picture.

SEYMOUR'S OF SHERBORNE. One of Seymour's lorries in the 1920s. Established in 1854,
this company made soft drinks in the works at the bottom of Bristol Road until 1990, when
they moved to larger premises in Wincanton. Standing in front are, from left to right: R. Park,
W. Hall, ? Godby.

THE BUS SERVICE, MILBORNE PORT c. 1925. This photograph shows the village's first bus to Sherborne and Yeovil parked at the weighbridge. This bus was an AEC Type YC that started life as a double-decker and was later re-bodied. The date of the conversion is unknown. The bus, still running in 1929, was owned by the National Omnibus and Transport Company of Yeovil and was garaged overnight in Winter's Yard, North Street.

THE DIGBY HOTEL COACH. When George Wingfield Digby built the Digby Hotel in 1869 he also provided this coach so that passengers alighting from the train at Sherborne Station could be transported to the hotel, despite it being only a very short walk!

A DAY TRIP, SHERBORNE 1920. One of Seager's fleet of charabancs provides the transport for a South Western Dairies staff outing, seen here setting out for the day in 1920. The driver, wearing the cap and white coat, is Mr Alan Seager and identified among the passengers are: Sidney, Ray and Mrs Dyke, John, Mabel and Rose Humphries, Abby Stickland, Bill Batterick and Reg Andrews.

THE RAILWAY, SHERBORNE. Between 1951 and 1954, Southern Region of British Railways built three diesel locomotives for the Waterloo-Exeter line. Here is No 10202 leaving the station in 1954. There is also a good view of the main gasholder with the Slopes in the background.

Acknowledgements

Special thanks are due to Gerald Pitman for his unstinting help, always freely given. Also to Fred Pearce, Nancy Pearce and Stanley McKay for passing on their intimate knowledge of Milborne Port, its history and its people. Also to Ann Smith for writing the introduction and her enthusiasm for this project. Our thanks go to the following people for information and permission to use photographs:

Mr D. Andrews, Mr R. Ansell, Miss M. Baker, Mr M. Baker, Mr P. Barter, Mr A. Baxter, Mrs M. Biss, Mrs R. Brown, Mrs N. Clarke, Mrs J. Cole, Mrs Q. Coles, Mr and Mrs A. Coney, Mr D. Coombs, Mr T.M. Coombs, Mr A.S. Darley, Mr E.W.G. Davis, Mr S. Wingfield Digby, Mr K. Dyke, Mrs M. Farnes, Mrs L. Foster, Mr D.R. Gear, Mr R.E. Gear, Mr R. Gosney, Mrs J. Gould, Mrs J. Habberfield, Mr G. Hallett, Mr M. Hatcher, Mr and Mrs J. House, Mr R.A. Hutchinson, Mr M. Johns, Mr and Mrs L. Kitzerow, Mr and Mrs R. Lickorish, Mrs D. Miller, Mr and Mrs P. Miller, Mr M. Nurton, Mrs J. Oxford, Mrs J. Parker, Mr J. Pike, Mrs M. Russell, Mrs J. Saunders, Mr L. Sharp, Mr G. Smith, Mr and Mrs D. Swift, Mrs L. Taylor, Mrs M. Tyler, Mrs E. Woodbridge and finally, to Mrs Jackie Freeman for producing the computer disc of the manuscript. We are especially grateful to our wives, Muriel and Theresa, for their help, advice, encouragement, forbearance and understanding, when the 'going' got tough!

Richard Duckworth would especially like to thank all those people in Milborne Port who have, over the years, contributed information about the village and offered photographs for his collection. He would welcome hearing from anyone who may have interesting photographs or stories to add to his archive of the village and its people.